Discharge Planning
Handbook
for Healthcare

Discharge Planning Handbook for Healthcare

Top 10 Secrets to Unlocking a New Revenue Pipeline

Ali Birjandi · Lisa M. Bragg

CRC Press
Taylor & Francis Group
Boca Raton   London   New York

CRC Press is an imprint of the
Taylor & Francis Group, an **informa** business

A PRODUCTIVITY PRESS BOOK

Productivity Press
Taylor & Francis Group
270 Madison Avenue
New York, NY 10016

International Standard Book Number-13: 978-1-56327-392-6 (Softcover)

Library of Congress Cataloging-in-Publication Data

Birjandi, Ali.
    Discharge planning handbook for healthcare : top 10 secrets to unlocking a new revenue pipeline / Ali Birjandi and Lisa M. Bragg.
        p. ; cm.
    Includes bibliographical references and index.
    ISBN 978-1-56327-392-6 (hardcover : alk. paper) 1. Health facilities--Discharge planning--Handbooks, manuals, etc. 2. Hospitals--Admission and discharge--Handbooks, manuals, etc. 3. Continuum of care--Handbooks, manuals, etc. I. Bragg, Lisa M. II. Title.
    [DNLM: 1. Patient Discharge--standards. 2. Efficiency, Organizational. 3. Patient Discharge--economics. 4. Quality Assurance, Health Care--methods. WX 158 B618d 2008]

RA971.8.B46 2008
362.11--dc22   2008012574

Visit the Taylor & Francis Web site at
http://www.taylorandfrancis.com

and the Productivity Press Web site at
http://www.productivitypress.com

Dedication

To Cameron, Jordan, and Aidan for allowing me to
finish this book without any major disasters.

ARB

To Bill, Brianna, and Billy, a special thanks and acknowledgment
for the sacrifices that each of you made in an effort to allow
the completion of this book. You have each inspired me
to work harder, focus more, and achieve.

LMB

Contents

Preface

Failure to recognize the overarching impact that proper discharge planning has on costs, operations, service, and quality of care, can cost your organization millions. Discharge planning is being forced to take on a new face in the world of healthcare and the choice to remain stagnant is no longer an option. The *Discharge Planning Handbook for Healthcare* is designed to provide new innovative solutions that can turn one of the most antiquated aspects of healthcare into one of the most productive. The theme of this book involves redefining discharge planning to realize hidden financial opportunities. The new performance-improvement concepts and approaches discussed balance all aspects of existing business models to provide a new approach to managing the discharge planning process. This book provides forward-thinking organizations with innovative tools that allow the user to perform ordinary functions in extraordinary ways. It is the authors' hope that by identifying a new revenue pipeline through improved discharge planning, a greater respect for this function can be achieved in the healthcare industry.

There is an abundance of information written on various types of discharge planning models (i.e., care coordination, case management, social work, utilization review, etc.). Because of the complexity of this function, the authors have chosen to focus this book on the administrative aspects of the process. This includes the case management, utilization review, and social work functions in an acute care setting. However, the purpose of this book is unique in that it provides not just a new approach, but also hidden secrets based on 25 years of discharge planning experience.

This book is intended for clinical and nonclinical hospital managers, directors, and officers. Specific discharge planning department team members such as case managers, care coordinators, utilization reviewers, and social workers will also find the information contained in this book highly applicable to their day-to-day processes. Further, healthcare students, physicians, and midlevel providers will gain insight to the depth and scope of the discharge planning function and its overarching impacts on costs, operations, service, and quality of care.

The *Discharge Planning Handbook for Healthcare* consists of five distinct concepts based on the Six Sigma DMAIC model (define, measure, analyze, improve, and control):

1. redefining discharge planning
2. focusing on the right metrics
3. using Lean concepts for redesign
4. using a practical approach for improvement
5. creating a culture that produces results

Readers will learn how to connect the discharge planning process with the continuous and relentless performance-improvement methodologies.

Chapters 1 and 2 begin with understanding the discharge planning function and the ability to identify opportunities for improvement. Chapters 3 and 4 help the reader focus on the right metrics to measure success. Chapter 5 details "Lean" methodologies for eliminating non-value-added tasks. Chapters 6 through 9 highlight the infrastructure required to transition to an optimal state of performance. Chapter 10 reviews the basic premise of Six Sigma methodologies in discharge planning, with the intent to show the practical aspects of the methodology through the Lean Six Sigma Action Workout. Chapter 11 discusses the importance of accountability, with an emphasis on achieving results. In the final chapter, the reader is provided a step-by-step implementation strategy for redesigning the discharge planning process to create a new revenue pipeline.

A case study is included to help readers utilize the basic concepts of the book in an interactive forum. The key provided in this case study will assist in measuring the reader's newly acquired skill sets. Additionally, a spreadsheet tool is provided to help users of this book to measure, improve, and maintain optimal costs, operations, service, and quality of care (COS-Q).

Acknowledgment

Special thanks and acknowledgments to Kathy Birjandi and Marry Jo Clark for their invaluable input and critical review of the book.

ARB and LMB

Introduction

Healthcare is characterized by fragmentation—among disciplines, among departments, among organizations, and among geographic locales—while those it serves depend on coordinated efforts. The system propagates waste—waste of time, resources, and goodwill.

The Institute of Medicine

In healthcare, no one understands this quote better than members of the discharge planning team. The impact of fragmented processes and wasted resources is a day-to-day reality. Compounding the problem is an underlying lack of awareness on the part of senior leadership in most organizations on the impact of improper discharge planning. Some organizations make the mistake of assuming that the function of discharge planning is the mere task of moving a patient from point A to point B. Rather, it should be viewed as a process that begins the minute the patient's admission becomes evident and ends when the patient is seamlessly transferred to the next level of care.

By underestimating the impact of discharge planning on costs, operations, service, and quality, many organizations miss the opportunity to control a critical component of the healthcare process. Understanding and controlling all of these steps is the key to a hidden revenue pipeline.

The Healthcare Landscape

Regulatory, market, and consumer forces have had a profound impact on the healthcare landscape in America. The rising cost of healthcare has surged to become the most significant cost pressure for U.S. businesses, resulting in over 40 million Americans joining the ranks of the uninsured. Additionally, the aging baby boomers are predicted to bankrupt Medicare by 2025 through increased utilization of services in an industry still recovering from the consolidation of the 1990s.

Hospitals are scrambling to maintain shrinking margins while, at the same time, attempting to conserve enough resources to meet the ever-changing demands of healthcare in America. Recent efforts to squeeze costs out of operating rooms and emergency departments are no longer enough to combat ever-decreasing commercial and governmental reimbursements. There is a strong necessity for healthcare institutions to reinvent existing business models as they move into the future. Survival in this "perfect storm" hinges on knowing how to minimize costs while finding new sources of revenue.

Past Drivers in Healthcare

In the last two decades, discharge planning departments have witnessed dramatic industry changes as a result of hospital downsizing, closures, and consolidations. These changes have impacted hospital performance in almost every department. Some of the most significant changes include:

- *Constrained capacity*: The Healthcare Advisory Board recently suggested that, based on a moderate growth scenario, hospital inpatient days will rise 3.5% each year through 2010, requiring a need to increase capacity by 40%.[1]
- *Overcrowded emergency departments (EDs)*: ED visits grew by 26% between 1993 and 2003. Over the same period, the number of EDs declined by 425, and the number of hospital beds declined by 198,000.[2]
- *Emergency department and hospital diversions*: Ambulances are frequently diverted from crowded EDs to other hospitals that may be farther away and may not have optimal services. In 2003, ambulances were diverted 501,000 times, an average of once every minute.[3]
- *Quality and service issues*: Consolidations have reduced the number of beds available, producing longer patient wait times. To combat these service issues, consumers have demanded transparency of hospital service indicators.
- *High readmission rates*: Nearly 18% of Medicare patients admitted to hospitals are readmitted within 30 days of discharge, accounting for $15 billon in spending.[4]

Hospitals across America are still recovering from the changes that occurred in the last decade. Many organizations have addressed the symptoms of the problem by increasing beds or implementing patient placement systems. Yet few have addressed the need to link the management of patient throughput and the management of resources to coordinate the transition of patients across different levels of care to unlock hidden capacity.

Future Drivers in Healthcare

There are many changes occurring today in the healthcare industry that will shape the structure of healthcare organizations in the next decade. Unlike the past, some of these drivers are independent of governmental or administrative control. There are five main issues that precipitate from these market forces:

1. The double-digit inflation in the cost of healthcare is taking a huge toll on the economy. For most businesses, healthcare costs are the single largest expense. In the next few years, this may force employers to select health plans that share risks with the employee.

2. The baby boomer retirees will begin draining the healthcare system in the next two decades, significantly impacting discharge planning departments. Government and health plan providers have already begun transitioning for this impact by increasing controls on standard criteria to justify acute care utilization and introducing pay for performance. The Hospital Quality Incentive Demonstration (HQID) pay-for-performance project (sponsored by the Centers for Medicare & Medicaid Services [CMS] and Premier, Inc.) is the first national pay-for-performance project of its kind. It is designed to determine whether financial incentives are effective at improving the quality of inpatient hospital care.[5] More than 260 hospitals are voluntarily participating in the project. The project's foundation for tracking hospital performance is Premier's Perspective™ database, the largest clinical comparative database in the nation.[6]

3. Transparency is a phenomenon that has only recently started to emerge within healthcare institutions. This is a broad-scale trend that enables consumers to compare the quality and price of healthcare services among different providers. It entails the public display of charges for service, adherence to quality standards and access to healthcare

scorecards for comparison. This forces hospitals to increase sensitivity to the demands of a consumer-driven market in the healthcare arena.

4. Decreasing reimbursement from payers and the erosion of public support have resulted in the reduction and elimination of hospital inpatient psychiatric units, as well as private and state behavioral health facilities.[7] This inadvertently requires an awareness of the discharge planning team to secure necessary resources for patients requiring psychiatric services at the time of discharge.

5. Nearly 46 million Americans have no health insurance coverage, including more than 9 million children.[8] Medicaid covers 57 million individuals, including 28 million children and nearly 9 million disabled citizens.[9] Many of these individuals lack a regular source of healthcare and look to community hospitals as their medical safety net.[10]

These changes in the healthcare environment clearly highlight the need to create proactive strategies to manage these issues. The market forces confronting the healthcare industry will force leadership to look at discharge planning as one of the most important resources within the organization. Together, these new drivers have created a looming "perfect storm" that can easily break the healthcare system in the United States, leaving businesses bankrupt and citizens uninsured. Knowing the secrets of an optimized discharge planning team is the key to maximizing profitability and ensuring survival.

Endnotes

1. Healthcare Advisory Board, *The New Economics of Care: Briefing for the Board and Health Systems Executives* (Washington: Advisory Board Company, fall 2001).
2. R. Martinez, T. Buchman, and M. Roizen, "Report Slams U.S. Emergency Care System," interview on *Talk of the Nation*, NPR, June 14, 2006. www.npr.org/templates/story/story.php?storyId=5485128.
3. Ibid.
4. L. Landro, "Keeping Patients from Landing Back in the Hospital," *The Wall Street Journal Online*, 2007.
5. Premier, Inc., "CMS/Premier Hospital Quality Demonstration," http://www.premierinc.com/quality-safety/tools-services/p4p/hqi/index.jsp.
6. Ibid.
7. American Hospital Association, "Prepare to Care," The Chartist Group, 2006.
8. Ibid.
9. Ibid.
10. Ibid.

Chapter 1

Discharge Planning Defined

When you change the way you look at things, the things you look at change.

Dr. Wayne Dyer

In this chapter, readers will learn:

- the definition of discharge planning
- key stakeholders in discharge planning departments
- team members of the discharge planning department
- discharge planning models
- COS-Q: the most important letters in optimizing discharge planning
- impacts of discharge planning departments on COS-Q
- the future state of discharge planning

Discharge Planning Defined

Medicare defines discharge planning as "a process used to decide what a patient needs for a smooth move from one level of care to another." Traditionally, this represented services to assist patients in arranging the care needed following a hospital stay. This included services for home care, nursing home care, rehabilitative care, outpatient medical treatment, and other assistance. Today, discharge planning is considered a process, not a single event. The process begins at admission and does not end until the patient is placed into the next level of care. Discharge from a hospital does not mean that a patient has fully recovered. It simply means that a physician has determined that the patient's condition is stable enough for the next level of care.

Discharge planning departments are commonly referred to as departments of case management, social work, care coordination, utilization review, or patient and family services. The professionals working in these departments are commonly licensed nurses or social workers. Viewed as an ancillary or supportive role, discharge planning by default has been viewed as a very reactive process. Its main focus has been on the seamless coordination of care as patients transitioned from the hospital to the next level of care.

The last two decades have changed the face of discharge planning. With ever-changing regulatory, market, and financial forces, discharge planning functions are in a state of perpetual change. Traditional tasks are quickly being replaced by processes that assist the organization in meeting regulatory compliance and maximizing reimbursement.

Key Stakeholders

In the last decade, administrators have come to realize that there are many more stakeholders involved in the discharge planning process. These include, but are not limited to, the following:

- family members
- discharge planning team members
- physicians and midlevel providers
- ancillary team members
- hospital business units
- health plans and providers
- post-acute care vendors
- the community at large

As the complexity of the discharge planning process increases, the number of stakeholders will continue to increase. Furthermore, as reimbursement and denials processes become more critical, changes in discharge planning processes will have a greater impact on each stakeholder.

Team Members of the Discharge Planning Department

A lead software project manager from ECIN® (Extended Care Information Network, now Allscripts) has stated, "If you have seen one Discharge Planning department, you have seen one Discharge Planning department." This comment underscores the fact that there are many job titles, department names, and divisions that have similar names and functions, each operating within variations of the discharge planning process.

There are many different job titles across hospitals in the U.S. healthcare systems. Additionally, the role of a team member can vary from hospital to hospital, making if very difficult to compare functions. This book will review the following team members: case managers, utilization-review persons, care coordinators, clinical documentation specialists or unit-based coding professionals, and social workers.

■ *Case managers* support the collaborative process of assessment, planning, facilitation, and advocacy for options and services to meet the patient's health needs. This role is focused on providing clinical oversight for a patient's care, managing and controlling length of stay, and serving as a liaison between physicians, patients, family members, and ancillary members of the healthcare team. Case managers often participate in the quality programs of the hospital and work to improve clinical outcomes through the development of clinical pathways and physician order sets. Clinical pathways, also known as critical paths, pathways, or care plans, are management plans that display goals for patients and provide the sequence and timing of actions necessary to achieve these goals with optimal efficiency.[1] As competition in the healthcare industry has increased, managers have embraced critical pathways as a method to reduce variation in care, decrease resource utilization, and potentially improve healthcare.[2] The case manager may also be involved in patient education and the tracking and trending of quality data. There are three common types of case managers: unit-based, disease-based, and physician-aligned.

1. *Unit-based case managers* are assigned to a specific unit(s) of a hospital and are focused on the clinical aspects of the patient's care. They provide oversight of the patient while the patient is receiving care in that specific unit. Their key purpose is to facilitate quality patient care during hospitalization of an assigned number of cases by managing, coordinating, and facilitating to achieve optimal

clinical outcomes in a timely, cost-effective manner. They are often viewed as a key member of the team, as they often have strong relationships with the ancillary team members of the unit.

2. *Disease-based case managers* are focused on a specific disease state or chronic complex condition. These case managers follow patients from admission to discharge and may also do prehospital teaching for scheduled or anticipated admissions. Disease-based case managers follow the patient to any unit in the hospital. In integrated delivery systems (IDSs), where transitional care units or post-acute care facilities are within the hospital, the disease-based case manager may also provide oversight for the patient in that setting. Since these team members are focused on a specific disease or on chronic complex conditions, they are required to have specialized knowledge and skills in an effort to deliver effective care.

3. *Physician-based case managers* are assigned to a physician or group practice. They may also follow a patient from admission to discharge, and may also do prehospital teaching for scheduled or anticipated admissions. Physician-based case managers follow the patient to any unit in the hospital where the physician or physician group has a patient. These team members are focused on creating a smooth transition for the patient from a clinical perspective. They also serve as a facilitator for the physician, assisting with navigation through the hospital. Depending on the credentials of the case manager, they may also provide patient education, assist with patient procedures, or assist the physician by preparing consents for surgical procedures. This case manager also serves as a liaison for the ancillary team members, patient, family members, and the physician office.

■ *Utilization review* is the assessment of how certain medical services are requested and performed. The review typically involves an admission review, a concurrent review or an inpatient evaluation of care and needs, or a retrospective review (post-discharge review of reasons for acute-care bed utilization and hospital services rendered). The utilization-review team member is a liaison between the hospital, physician, and health plan. This process is accomplished by applying standard guidelines that determine medical necessity for the use of hospital resources. These guidelines are used by health plans in making determinations regarding reimbursement for the hospital stay. Utilization-review experts must understand the clinical aspects of the patients' conditions, be familiar with the standard criteria utilized, and be aware of commercial and governmental health plan guidelines. The crux of a hospital reimbursement rests on the ability of the utilization-review team members to understand and articulate the medical necessity of the patient's episode of care. This team member must be well-versed in payer regulations and guidelines and the associated impact on average length of stay (ALOS) and reimbursement.

■ *Care coordinators* are nurses or social workers who perform the combined function of a case manager and utilization review. This function manages both the clinical and financial oversight of a patient's episode of care. This role may also include Core Measure review, patient education, and serving as a liaison for the staff nurses and ancillary team members. In some circumstances, the care coordinator role serves as a combined function of case management, utilization review, and clinical documentation functions.

■ *Clinical documentation specialists or unit-based coding professionals* are team members who concurrently review the medical record in an effort to ensure that the physician documentation accurately reflects the resources needed to care for the patient. They are specifically concerned with health plans that reimburse based on diagnosis-related groups (DRGs). DRGs are a patient-classification system that relates types of patient treatment to resources consumed. The goal of this function is to capture the appropriate documentation of the physician to ensure that reimbursement matches the disease burden and resource consumption.

■ *Social workers* have the dynamic role of coordinating many tasks for a patient during some of the most critical stages in a patient's life. Hospital social workers are licensed personnel who assess the psychosocial needs of a patient and then develop, implement, and evaluate the discharge plan. A social worker provides support, counseling, and education of community-based services for the patient and family members. They serve as a key facilitator assisting with many services, which can include obtaining guardianship, facilitating an adoption, and addressing abuse/neglect issues. Other responsibilities may include acting as an advocate to assist the patient with community resources, providing information about indigent drug programs, and setting up transportation services. They are also responsible for the coordination of a patient's transition from one level of care to the next.

Job Title	Dyad Model 1	Dyad Model 2	Dyad Model 3
Utilization Review	√		
Care Coordinator (Utilization Review and Case Management Functions)		√	
Care Coordinator (Utilization Review, Case Management, and CDMP Function)			√
Social Worker	√	√	√
Unit-based Coding Professional	√*	√*	

* denotes team members that may integrate with the model

Figure 1.1   Dyad functional model

Discharge Planning Models

There are a number of different discharge planning models that are used across the country. The two most common models are the Dyad and the Triad. While there are many different variations of these two models (see Figure 1.1 and Figure 1.2), there is little research identifying which model and staffing configuration yields the best outcomes. However, there are certain advantages and disadvantages to each model that will be discussed further in Chapter 6.

1. The Dyad model involves utilizing a care coordinator and a social worker. The care coordinator performs both utilization-review and case-management functions, thus providing clinical oversight and review of the case for medical-necessity criteria. The care coordinator serves as a liaison for the patient and family members, physician,

Job Title	Triad Model 1	Triad Model 2	Triad Model 3	Triad Model 4	Triad Model 5	Triad Model 6
Case Manager – Unit-based	√	√				
Case Manager – Disease-based			√	√		
Case Manager – Physician-based					√	√
Utilization Review	√		√		√	
Care Coordinator (Utilization Review and CDMP Functions)		√		√		√
Social Worker	√	√	√	√	√	√
Unit-based Coding Professional	√*		√*		√*	

* denotes team members that may integrate with the model

Figure 1.2   Triad functional model

ancillary team members, and health-plan administrators. The social worker performs the psychosocial and continuum-of-care functions.

2. In a Triad model, three main functions exist: a case manager (any of the three discussed), a utilization-review nurse, and a social worker. In this model, the care manager is focused on the clinical aspects of the patient's episode of care. As noted, this function involves the development of clinical pathways or best-practice standards of care and education to the patient. The case manager is also responsible for Core Measure review or quality. This team member serves as a clinical "gap-filler," providing strong clinical oversight for patients and assisting bedside nurses with day-to-day management of the patient in an effort to minimize length of stay. The utilization-review nurse reviews the medical record for medical necessity and manages commercial and governmental requirements. The social worker addresses the psychosocial aspects of the patient and identifies discharge planning

needs. Once needs are identified, the social worker implements the plan and assists with preparing any necessary documentation required.

There has been a shift in many facilities to add a new support function called care coordinator assistants or social work assistants. These functions generally perform clerical functions such as preparing discharge planning packets, faxing referral forms, making phone calls, and data entry.

In a recent article in *Professional Case Management,* Sandra M. Terra attempted to determine whether there is adequate evidence-based justification for selection of one acute-care model over another. Her research identified no fewer than five models and four to six submodels. The study illustrated the following:[3]

- Regardless of disease condition, the effectiveness of the model results in increased quality of care, decreased ALOS, increased patient and physician satisfaction, and creates a better care continuum when there is direct patient contact by the team member.
- Preferred models result in measurable outcomes that can be directly related to and demonstrate alignment with organizational strategy.
- Case management or care coordination does reduce cost, decrease ALOS, and improve outcomes.
- Integrated models that involve both social workers and nurses are the most effective models in an acute care case-management setting.
- The successful model recognizes physicians and patients as valued customers and part of the partnership, which creates an environment that affects financial outcomes.
- A successful model also reduces the length of stay and improves the quality and delivery of care as well as patient and physician satisfaction.

COS-Q: The Most Important Letters in Optimizing Discharge Planning

Discharge planning departments have emerged as fundamental components of the healthcare system, effective at impacting hospital costs, operations, service, and quality. These departments can no longer be viewed as "cost centers" but, rather, as valuable assets that can drive bottom-line results. The secret to harnessing the synergy of the discharge planning team is to create a new focus. Breakthrough performance must embrace a focused and balanced approach toward managing costs, operations, service, and quality indicators. Together, these variables are known as the **COS-Q**. This acronym represents the department's ability to manage the following:

- *Cost* and resource consumption
- *Operations* by ensuring productivity and efficiency, hence optimization
- *Service* and satisfaction of the customer
- *Quality* of care

When the focus of the discharge planning department is aimed at balancing COS-Q, favorable results are inevitable. In today's healthcare market, managing COS-Q needs to be ingrained into the culture so that team members are not simply managing tasks, but managing tasks with a purpose. That purpose is to improve the COS-Q.

Impacts of Discharge Planning on COS-Q

There are five main process steps that occur when a patient enters the hospital (see Figure 1.3):

1. Admission/registration
2. Diagnostic workup/procedure
3. Evaluation of condition and plan
4. Evaluation of discharge readiness
5. Discharge and transition for follow-up

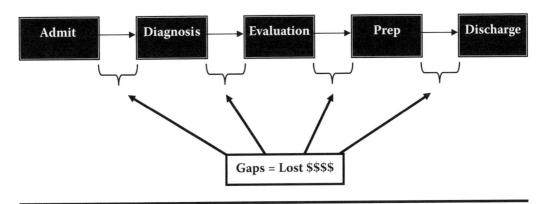

Figure 1.3   Clinical episode of care process map

Figure 1.3 demonstrates potential gaps in service that patients experience during their hospital stay. In an optimal setting, as the patient's episode of care begins, discharge planning is initiated within 24 hours of the admission. As the stay progresses, there will be continuous gaps in service; however, not all gaps can be diminished. Each opportunity to lessen the amount of time it takes to get from one process to the next can reduce unnecessary costs, collectively saving millions of dollars.

When gaps in the process are not minimized, inefficiencies are maximized. These gaps or delays in service produce an upstream tidal wave of patient-flow constraints, which negatively impact costs, operations, service, and quality. Strengthening the focus of the discharge planning team in conjunction with increasing their awareness of the financial and clinical components associated with patient throughput can add significant value to the organization.

Hospitals that fail to recognize the strong relationship that discharge planning departments have on the revenue cycle are missing considerable opportunities to improve bottom-line results. With each admission, part of the revenue cycle is triggered. Figure 1.4 demonstrates the administrative functions that are managed during a patient's episode of care. The figure depicts three stages: prehospitalization, hospitalization, and posthospitalization.

During the prehospitalization period, a number of events can occur. These events include obtaining demographic data and insurance information, and notification to the health plan of a scheduled admission. During the hospitalization period, nursing, physician, discharge planning, and ancillary services are occurring. During the posthospitalization period, the billing cycle is in process. In an integrated delivery system, this would also trigger the beginning of the revenue cycle for post-acute-care services. Each of the periods is associated with a number of variables that impact the revenue pipeline.

Although this diagram may be oversimplified, it is important to note the significance of the middle section. This serves as the connector between the prehospitalization and posthospitalization portions of the pipeline. The discharge planning department, if positioned correctly, is the common thread linking the administrative and clinical components of a patient's episode of care. The better hospitals become at understanding this relationship, the better the COS-Q.

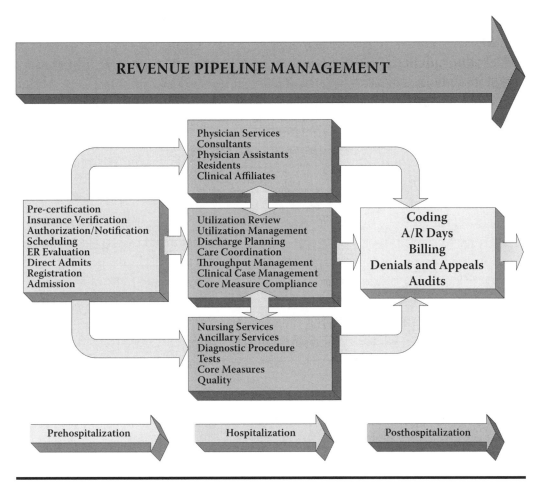

Figure 1.4   Discharge planning relationship to the revenue cycle

The Future State of Discharge Planning

As hospitals position for the future, the complexity of healthcare will force members of the discharge planning team to become part of the internal leverage required to impact the following:

- *Control average length of stay (ALOS)*, and therefore costs
- *Improve patient throughput* by increasing bed turnover and reducing costly diversions
- *Assist with capacity management*, thus increasing revenue by revealing hidden capacity
- *Assure medical necessity*, thereby securing appropriate and timely reimbursement

- *Assure governmental and payer compliance*, thereby avoiding payment denial
- *Secure concurrent documentation*, which will improve quality and optimize the rate of reimbursement
- *Improve customer service*, thereby increasing market share
- *Promote services* by generating referrals back to the company or affiliated partners.
- *Improve coordination of the discharge*, thereby reducing readmit rates and improving physician, patient, and payer satisfaction.

Discharge planning becomes effective when team members understand the favorable contributions that can be made. Managing the people, creating the right processes, and providing the necessary tools (technology) will be key to unlocking a hidden revenue pipeline. Hospitals must change their approach to adapt to the ever-changing environment. While it is not always an easy journey, the status quo is no longer an option.

References

1. S. D. Pearson, D. Goulart-Fisher, and T. H. Lee, "Critical Pathways as a Strategy for Improving Care: Problems and Potential," *Ann. Intern. Med.* 123 (1995): 941–948.
2. Ibid., 123.
3 S. M. Tara, "The Evidence Based Approach to a Case Management Model Selection for an Acute Case Facility: Is There Really a Preferred Model?" *Professional Case Manage.* 12, no. 3 (May–June 2007): 147–157.

Chapter 2

How Optimized Is Your Current Model?

To be conscious that you are ignorant is a great step to knowledge.

Benjamin Disraeli

In this chapter, readers will learn:

- 12 key elements of an optimized discharge planning department
- how to benchmark correctly
- why hospitals should optimize and not maximize

Before any organization can begin its journey, it must know from where it is starting. It is this critical step that creates the foundation for the "buy-in" required to take people, processes, and technology through a transformational journey. Arming yourself with critical information about your organization's COS-Q (cost, operations, service, and quality of care) allows the appropriate management of variables that will guide a project toward a future vision. Identifying and capturing the relevant data, analyzing it correctly, and converting it into actionable intelligence is the key to adapting within the current healthcare environment.

The standards used to measure the effectiveness and efficiency of discharge planning systems have evolved over time. This is a consequence of changing federal regulations, market pressures, consumerism, and financial constraints. As these forces change the landscape of healthcare, the business intelligence used to manage them will also change.

Because the discharge planning functions in today's acute-care facilities are complex, it is difficult to assess any organization or system without a thorough evaluation of COS-Q. There are, however, several key elements in any discharge planning system that will flag optimal vs. suboptimal performance. These variables differentiate a good discharge planning system from a great one. They include:

- standard tools for improvement
- efficient process flow
- technology utilization
- efficient communication patterns
- interactive vs. reactive discharge planning
- transparency and accountability
- access to business intelligence
- staff productivity
- clinical quality
- financial performance
- customer service
- benchmarking

Key Elements of an Optimized Discharge Planning Department

Standardized Tools

Optimized organizations use a standardized toolset for Performance Improvement (PI). Standardized tools optimize the effectiveness of change, boost efficiency in performing tasks, and can save time and money. Using a standardized methodology forces the utilization of the most effective tools for staff members who may not be familiar with business process reengineering. By documenting and educating staff on the PI process, organizations can expect to impact the culture over time. In doing so, adapting to a new business environment becomes an integral part of the job as opposed to adopting a series of discrete initiatives.

Traditionally, most organizations have used a myriad of tools and processes for the PI life cycle. Organizations have been inundated with tool sets for assessment, feasibility, implementation, and benefits realization.

Although many of these tools have been used for years, it is only in the last two decades that healthcare has begun to embrace most of them.

Common tools used for problem assessment and solutions development predominantly came from the Total Quality Management (TQM) and Continuous Quality Improvement (CQI) movements of the 1980s and 1990s. These tools have been in use in manufacturing industries for many years. To measure the feasibility of solutions, most organizations used time-tested financial indicators such as break-even and return on investment (ROI). For implementation, there have been very few set standards until the early 1990s. Today, there is the Project Management Institute (PMI), which certifies professional project managers in its methodology. Many organizations have made it a requirement for project managers to have this certification before instigating large-scale changes such as the implementation of a new discharge planning system. Benefits realization is a growing concept in healthcare. As projects become more expensive, outcome validation becomes more important.

The methodology that is increasingly becoming the standard tool of choice across most healthcare organizations is called Six Sigma. Six Sigma combined with the concepts of Lean (called Lean Six Sigma) provides a complete tool set for any organization to utilize a standardized approach toward change enablement. The Lean Six Sigma approach uses a process that takes the initiative through the entire project lifecycle. Organizations that do not have a consistent approach to develop, implement, and measure new solutions are considered suboptimized. We will discuss this methodology in further detail in Chapter 5 and Chapter 10.

Efficient Process Flow

Optimized organizations have processes that are Lean and flow smoothly. Organizations that have the most streamlined processes consistently demonstrate a superior ability to manage COS-Q. Discharge planning processes must be designed to take full advantage of facility logistics, technology, and human capital. It is important to note that smooth processes are not always a function of new technology. Often it is the existing processes that must be streamlined before technology is implemented. For example, if a process produces a delayed length-of-stay (LOS) for a patient because of improper documentation, automating that process may not yield a different result. However, making processes flow smoothly by eliminating tasks that do not add value, and then enhancing that process with automation, can produce significant results.

In many discharge planning departments, the first step in the analysis is an assessment of work flow. This process can be further developed into a Value Map (discussed in Chapter 5) to provide more detail about each task. Often, at the end of the analysis, opportunities precipitate from potential consolidation, automation, and/or elimination of tasks. One quick way of evaluating the processes in a system is to ask the following questions:

■ Are the tasks in the process adding value to the people served (i.e., customer satisfaction)?
■ Are the tasks in the process adding value to the operations (i.e., ability to deliver services)?
■ Are the tasks in the process non-value-added (i.e., can they be eliminated or changed without harming service levels or the organization)?

The flow of information is as important as the logistical flow of team members and patients. In measuring a good process flow, it is critical to understand how the information is being gathered and how it is being distributed. A common non-value-added step in discharge planning is documentation. Often team members perform double and triple documentation of information taken from the medical record of the patient. For example, a nurse enters data into the patient's chart, that information is copied by case managers, then by a utilization-review nurse, then by a social worker. Redundant documentation is a non-value-added step in the discharge planning process. Discharge planning departments that exhibit more than 20% of time performing non-value-added or redundant processes are considered inefficient. Optimized departments strive for elimination of all non-value-added steps.

High-performing organizations consistently utilize best practices from other organizations to continuously improve their own processes. Benchmarking companies (such as Thomson Healthcare's Action O-I Operational Benchmarking) provide data-sharing agreements among other like facilities. This provides a direct comparison with other organizations, and an opportunity for exchange of information on both processes that have succeeded and those that have failed. Organizations that streamline work flow and consistently benchmark for best practices on an ongoing basis are, without fail, the highest performing institutions.

Technology Utilization

In a recent survey, 70% of all discharge planning departments in the Midwest were using some type of process automation technology. Although relatively new in healthcare, discharge planning technologies can reduce paper, eliminate duplication, improve communication between stakeholders, and automate tasks. It is very difficult to have a high-performing discharge planning department that functions without the utilization of automated technologies.

By eliminating time-consuming tasks, technology by default increases the productivity of the staff. It is not uncommon to see caseloads increase by 10–20% with the advent of new automated systems. Additionally, an organization can expect to remove over 90% of paper through the use of technology. A litmus test of efficiency with new automation technology is the amount of paper that is generated per patient in the performance of daily tasks.

These automated systems impact all metrics in the COS-Q. For example, patient placement systems offer applications that connect hospitals, outpatient facilities, and service providers throughout the patient care continuum, thus making the process of managing referrals and placing a patient more secure, effective, and timely. This increases service by providing timely results, improves operations by reducing paperwork, decreases costs by quickly placing the patient in an appropriate setting, and improves quality by providing all options to the patient every time.

Most clinical technology vendors today provide department specific systems. Vendors of Electronic Medical Record (EMR) systems are advancing functionality to become a "single source" solution. These solutions are attractive to hospitals because a single vendor is able to integrate multiple technology needs across the company. Therefore, in the next decade it is anticipated that EMR vendors will buy out existing discharge planning technology solutions or will develop new platforms within their existing EMRs to automate the discharge planning function.

As discussed in detail in Chapter 9, organizations that optimize processes before the introduction of automated technologies are positioned to take full advantage of the new tools. If technology simply automates existing poor processes, the department is doomed to operate in a suboptimal state. Discharge planning departments that desire to take full advantage of technology are encouraged to consider optimizing work-flow processes before automating them.

Efficient Communication Systems

Most discharge planning functions are complex and require a significant amount of communication to operate. This complexity is a function of all stakeholders in the process who play a part in processing the patient through to a successful discharge. The amount of communication is massive on any scale. For example, it is not inconceivable to involve the case manager, social worker, utilization-review staff, unit clerk, bedside nurse, technologists, therapists, physicians, and the family in a single case. Organizations that effectively manage this communication between entities are considered optimized.

Although it is difficult, failure to manage communication properly can negatively impact the COS-Q through such metrics as missed discharges, physician/patient dissatisfaction, and billing errors. Critical points of communication include:

■ *Staff to patient and family*: It is critical to keep the patient and family informed during the entire patient stay on a daily basis. Many discharges have been delayed based on poor communication, resulting in an increased average length of stay (ALOS) and poor service. The inclusion of the family in the communication process becomes especially critical when the patient is elderly or very young. Generally, communication tends to increase as the discharge date draws closer. In optimized organizations, communication occurs even after discharge for service review and follow-up.

■ *Staff to physician*: Providing the right information at the right time to the physician is a major hurdle in coordinating the discharge process. Since most physicians are not under the same time constraint as the organization to discharge the patient, it is imperative that the staff have the right information at the right time to prevent any delays. Optimized organizations take advantage of time with the physician by anticipating issues prior to the physician's arrival.

■ *Staff to ancillary services*: Services such as respiratory care and rehabilitation care must coordinate all events to comply with all of the clinical requirements of the patient's stay. Setting daily rounds is the general practice for communicating the status of the patient for each service.

The mode of communication can occur in many ways between these entities. It could be face-to-face, phone calls, e-mails, patient chart, or via the computer. Most organizations use a combination of these methods. Discharge planning departments with the least communication problems have a tendency to leverage technology to its full advantage. High-performance organizations use all available resources to communicate efficiently and effectively.

Interactive vs. Reactive Organizations

Optimized organizations have discharge planning functions that begin managing the patient's stay as soon as an event has been identified. This process may begin before admission and end at final discharge from a post-acute-care setting based on the type of healthcare system. In interactive models, the key elements of a stay are monitored and linked into the process. Interactive departments use tools such as the "day before discharge" checklist to prepare the patient for discharge. This is contrary to the traditional management of patient discharge, which meant assisting the patient with leaving the organization on the day of discharge.

For optimized organizations, being interactive goes beyond anticipating the next step in the process. It also includes anticipating the decision points of providers to assist in the process. Discharge planning team members are in a unique position to bring all the information together to paint a picture of the patient's stay and, ultimately, find the best path that produces the optimal discharge for the patient.

Because of regulatory, financial, and market constraints, optimized organizations treat every discharge interactively. This allows the staff to identify every opportunity in advance to improve the COS-Q.

Transparency

As introduced in Chapter 1, transparency provides consumers with the ability to compare providers based on quality and cost. This is a relatively new phenomenon that allows patients to make more-informed decisions. At this time, the federal government only requires that organizations "report" this information, though there is pending legislation that will connect reimbursements with scores under a program commonly referred to as "pay-for-performance" (PFP). This is the federal government's strategy to provide healthcare institutions with an incentive for optimized performance.

Although initially led by the U.S. government, an increasing number of large payers such as Blue Cross/Blue Shield and Kaiser Permanente are leading the way to PFP. The momentum is gathering speed as more and more healthcare systems join this initiative. Organizations that are optimized are currently preparing to operate in an environment that can survive in a PFP world.

Another aspect of transparency is the sharing of information among all staff and physicians to promote an environment of openness. This new forum for staff allows quick identification of issues and resolutions across the facility, and will ultimately allow organizations to adapt to changes in a more efficient manner.

In order to operate in an open forum with staff, clear lines of responsibility and expectations have to be developed. The pressure is on management to create systems that are clear and consistent. Organizations that are optimized provide all information (good or bad) in an open environment.

Accountability

Optimized organizations develop standards and hold staff accountable to them. The alternative to this was the environment of the 1990s, when it was commonplace to hear of technology projects that failed because of unrealized benefits. The root cause of this dilemma was that few organizations held staff accountable to achieve the business objectives after go-live. A good measure of success is not whether the technology is functioning, but rather whether the benefits are achieved.

There are specific techniques and processes that managers must employ to develop the discipline in discharge planning departments to create a climate of accountability. With accountability, the staff usually performs better, since both the expectations and consequences are clear. This helps to ensure that there is equity among staff members, but it also helps reduce uncertainty by providing quick and specific feedback on performance. Optimized organizations encourage their staff to become more accountable through management behaviors. These two management policies (transparency and accountability) reinforce an environment that promotes openness and challenges the staff to meet targets. Together they provide a powerful combination to promote optimized performance.

Business Intelligence

Information is power. It is the key to the success and continued viability of every organization. If a process cannot be measured, then it cannot

Table 2.1 COS-Q Model

COSTS	*OPERATIONS*
These are key financial metrics that impact the bottom line. This includes indicators such as denials, cost by diagnosis-related group (DRG), margins on referrals, etc.	These are indicators that show system efficiency. These include indicators such as ALOS, average length of discharge (ALOD), number of referrals, full-time equivalent (FTE) per case, etc.
SERVICE	*QUALITY*
These are customer-service scores as defined by both patients and physicians. This includes indicators such as patient and physician satisfaction.	These are clinical measures that generally impact the patient care. This includes indicators such as Core Measures, readmit rates, etc.

be managed. By transforming data into knowledge, and knowledge into informed decisions, business intelligence can deliver the sophisticated analysis and insight that managers need to make sound business decisions. Yet, as many healthcare organizations have found, the information needed to engage staff, make strategic decisions, and demonstrate accountability is often scattered throughout multiple departments and databases. The ability of an organization to overcome this challenge by tying together disparate data sources to provide a cross-organizational view of vital information is what differentiates organizations that have optimal performance from those that do not.

In capturing actionable business intelligence, most organizations have leaned heavily on technology for real-time reports. The caveat is that too much technology in an organization can produce a wealth of data and little actionable intelligence. Hence, organizations are often caught in a "data rich" but "information poor" (DRIP) environment. It is critical to focus on metrics that have a direct impact on COS-Q. Every effort should be put toward those variables that are the most important to manage the discharge planning functions.

There are many models that help managers organize and prioritize operational metrics for efficiency and effectiveness. The best way to begin the data collection process is to break down the types of data required to manage the discharge planning function. It is imperative that each organization capture a balanced set of metrics that represent the stakeholders in the system. The COS-Q model is based on the report-card methodology and separates key measures into four quadrants: Cost (financial), Operations, Service, and Quality (see Table 2.1).

Together, these categories demonstrate a balanced picture of all the metrics required for PI. It is often tempting to look at only a single category of metrics, such as quality. But "value" is a compilation of cost, quality, service, and operations. The stakeholders in today's healthcare environment are becoming smarter and have higher expectations across all these categories. For example, no patient is willing to ask for the highest quality of care if that extra margin of quality means bankrupting his or her family.

Labor Productivity

Staff productivity is a key indicator of optimized discharge planning functions. Environments that show high productivity ratios are able to produce more output with fewer resources. It is imperative to note that quality and service have to be constant when assessing the value of increased productivity. Lower cost at the expense of lower quality or decreased customer satisfaction does not add value to the process, unless the affected variable(s) is perceived as non-value-add by the customer.

Generally, labor productivity is measured by worked hours per output. This can also be measured by Full-Time Equivalents (FTE), and Worked Hours Per Patient Day (WHPPD). Some of these productivity indicators can be complex and difficult to calculate. For example, the components of paid FTEs may include overtime and other premium pays. Not knowing what is included can skew any comparisons. A more practical approach is to use basic indicators that can be measured on the fly by staff. Below are a few indicators that are commonly used in optimized organizations to measure the output of employees in the discharge planning functions:

1. *Number of cases by care coordinators*: This is a staff productivity measure that gauges the output of staff in terms of both new and follow-up cases. These productivity standards need to be measured across all discharge planning functions, such as discharge planners, case managers, utilization review, and social workers. A helpful tool is a Min/Avg/Max chart to better identify the variation in staff productivity. Most PI targets are generally set to move staff operating at "Min" to "Avg."
   - Optimal organizations keep the number of cases at 20–25. Through the utilization of automated technologies, case loads can be increased to 25–30.

2. *Cases opened/closed*: This indicator measures the number of cases opened and the number of cases closed during a certain period of time. This information helps to identify any variation in the flow of patients into a unit, outflow of patients through discharges, and the match between labor and demand. Based on the difficulty of the patients in the unit, a Relative Value Unit (RVU) can be created to develop departmental Workload Units (WLU). These workload units set the standard for budgeting labor annually. It is important to account for the fact that this process is real-time and that the analysis is a snapshot at a particular place in time. Thus cases that were opened in one report may be closed in another report. The value of this product is in the tendency to show patterns that are developing.

   – If more cases are being opened than closed during a period of time, then managers should investigate the causes and potentially ask for more resources. If more cases are being closed than opened, then managers may potentially want to staff down to increase productivity per staff. For example, if too many patients are not being seen because of high census, management might consider shifting staff to weekends using overtime temporarily to even out the cases closed to cases opened.

3. *Percent of patients reviewed*: This metric is used for identifying the percent of patients not reviewed for case management, utilization, or social work opportunities. This metric measures both patients not seen during their entire stay, and the number of times that a patient was seen during his or her stay. For example, a patient may be seen once every three days, while another patient may be considered not critical enough to be seen at all. The issue that most organizations run into is that, with an average length of stay of 4.5 days, a patient may be discharged before the next visit.

   – Optimized organizations review 100% of patients every day. Although patients can be prioritized, this should be the goal.

4. *Time required to process a patient*: This is an excellent productivity metric that measures the amount of time it takes to process a patient by FTE in the Care Coordination department. The key is to compare staff members against each other to identify variations. This metric is a simple calculation based on total patients completed at the end of the day divided by the number of hours worked.

   – In a paper-based process, a utilization-review function can take an average of 20 minutes. This can be reduced to 10–15 minutes through the use of technology. The surplus labor can be used for other functions, such as increased percentage of patients seen or shifting staff to weekend coverage.

5. *FTE per discharge*: In order to calculate this metric, the number of FTEs for the department is divided by the number of discharges that occurred annually. This metric is important because utilization can be compared across floors, facilities, and other external organizations. Each metric should be split across utilization review, case management, discharge planning, and social work functions. Organizations that have a high number of patient transfers experience a lower FTE per discharge ratio. As a benchmark, most organizations experience three transfers per patient during the stay.
   - Optimized organizations trend at about 1 FTE in the Care Coordination department per 600 discharges.

6. *FTE per adjusted occupied bed*: This is another operational indicator that measures the productivity of staff. It utilizes the number of beds as the indicator for performance in labor productivity. This metric is generally adjusted for patient acuity or outpatient volumes for an apples-to-apples comparison.
   - It is important to know how this measure is being adjusted when benchmarking across organizations.

Quality Metrics

No discharge planning department can claim to be optimized if the clinical care provided for the patients is considered suboptimal. The quickest way to measure the process of care is through the government's standard Core Measures. Core Measures track a variety of evidence-based, scientifically researched process standards of care that have been shown to result in improved clinical outcomes for patients. CMS (Centers for Medicare & Medicaid Services) established Core Measures in 2000 and began publicly reporting data relating to Core Measures in 2003. The Web site for updated information is at http://www.cms.hhs.gov. Currently, there are 26 Core Measures spread over four areas: Heart Failure (HF), Acute Myocardial Infarction (AMI), Community Acquired Pneumonia (CAP), and Surgical Care Improvement Project (SCIP). Optimized organizations have been able to balance operational and financial constraints against quality indicators. Optimized discharge planning functions produce Core Measure indicators that are above the national standards.

Financial Performance

Costs or financial indicators generally measure the financial viability of the organization. These metrics are generally tied into increasing margins and tracking any variation that could potentially impact budgets. Optimized organizations should measure:

1. *Avoidable days*: This is a very basic financial metric that shows the number of days that could have been avoided during a patient's stay based on medical necessity. This metric is calculated as the number of days allowed (based on medical necessity) subtracted from actual patient days. It is important to note that each avoidable day can equate to a savings of about $300 to $500 per day, not including the opportunity cost of new patient revenues.

2. *Average denials*: This metric measures the number and dollar amount of denials that occurred based on medical necessity. Although there are many kinds of denials, it is imperative to measure only those that the discharge planning process has control over. For example, denials based on delayed payment is a billing issue, not a utilization-review (UR) issue, while denials based on medical necessity are a UR issue. This metric needs to be assessed with outliers removed so that isolated cases can be differentiated from consistent patterns.

3. *Types of referral to post-acute-care services*: This metric tracks the types of referrals being made to post-acute-care facilities. This includes services such as home health, rehab, hospice, etc. It is imperative that these metrics be constantly monitored to track referrals as a percent of discharges to identify any variations. This metric for most organizations should be between 20% to 30% based on acuity.

4. *Referrals by employee*: This is an important metric to track any employees that may be skewing the referral patterns. Anomalies are quickly identified and brought to the attention of management for a resolution.

5. *Average cost per FTE*: This metric trends labor costs over a period of time. It is imperative that labor costs for employees stay in tune with other like-employees in the organization. Often nurses are treated differently when they transition into a care-coordination model. High labor costs indicate either excessive overtime and premium pay, or excessive compensation packages. It is important to break down this metric into nursing and non-nursing.

6. *Dollars and volumes of ancillary service/product placement at discharge*: This metric measures the amount of secondary services provided for the patient at the point of discharge. This includes any durable medical equipment (DME) requirements and any post-acute-care service appointments for physician or diagnostic services.

Customer Service

These indicators measure service-level perceptions across all stakeholders. It is imperative to note that this includes the service to the patients, physicians, family, and even other clinicians who are part of the patient team. These metrics are generally measured in aggregate by Human Resources (HR) or the quality department through third-party organizations to prevent discrimination.

1. *Proper patient education at the point of discharge*: Measures patient satisfaction with the information provided at the point of discharge. Many organizations have started to complete this process by calling patients the day after the discharge for any follow-up.
2. *Proper communication with patient's family about discharge*: This indicator measures the perception of the patient regarding the communication of the staff with the family regarding the treatment and discharge planning process.
3. *Timely discharge*: Measures the perception of the patient regarding the consistency in the process. Did the discharge occur at the time that it was originally communicated?
4. *Proper communication with provider*: This is the provider's perception of the patient's status both in terms of the patient's condition and the discharge process during the patient encounter. This communication is measured for both the attending and the primary care provider (PCP). In many organizations, there is no mechanism to communicate with any physicians other than the attending.

Benchmarking

Comparing the organization's COS-Q to that of external entities is the key for identification and prioritization of opportunities. Without external benchmarking, it is nearly impossible to know if an organization's metrics are superior or inferior to others. It can be compared to "grading on a curve" for an exam. A score of 99% may sound spectacular, but not if everyone else received 100%. Benchmarking not only helps show the weaknesses in your COS-Q, but it also helps prioritize the functions that have the most opportunity for benefits.

There are many sources of benchmarking data. Horizontally integrated systems often benchmark against their own organizations. There are also benchmarking memberships available through vendors such as Solucient or Premier. Benchmarking companies are the best sources of data, since the data is automatically scrubbed and normalized in the compare groups for an "apples-to-apples" comparison. Other sources for benchmarking information include consulting companies and Internet-based niche surveyors.

There are two important factors that determine whether an organization's COS-Q is being benchmarked appropriately. Although no two organizations are the same, the *compare group*, and the *target opportunity* are the keys to ensuring that the benchmarking data is actionable.

In determining a good compare group, it is imperative that each organization complete a profile that best differentiates the characteristics of that organization. This could include case mix, bed size, teaching status, major service lines (i.e., oncology), rural/urban, tertiary/nontertiary, trauma levels, etc. By creating a profile that filters out organizations in the compare group that are not similar, the organizations in your compare group become more and more comparable to your own. The trap generally occurs when an organization inputs too many criteria attempting to create the perfect match, thus dropping the number of organizations in the compare group to below six. At this point, the data is statistically susceptible to high variation, introducing error rates and potentially false opportunities.

Another approach that many organizations use to develop good compare groups is the static method. In this method, organizations are hand-picked from the benchmarking pool that management feels best represent similar organizations. Unfortunately, being able to hand-pick the compare group is a function of those organizations being part of the pool. *The trap in this method is that management may opt to pull together a compare group that by default shows them to be favorable.*

The second factor that impacts the ability of an organization to benchmark correctly is the compare group target opportunity. In this process, a target is developed for the organization to achieve. If the organization chooses a very difficult target (i.e., top 25%), then the challenges could be insurmountable and morale may drop. On the other hand, if the target is set too low, then the benefits of improving to the organization's full potential are not realized, and the organization is at risk. *The optimal target is one that balances the environmental drivers with the culture of the organization.* Most organizations use 10% of the budget annually as a realistic target for improvement.

Maximized vs. Optimized

Knowing the difference between a maximized model and an optimized model is critical. In a maximized model, all interacting variables are individually maximized with the notion that "more is better." Counteracting this principle is the "law of diminishing returns." This law states that if input in the production of a commodity is increased while all other inputs are held fixed, a point will eventually be reached at which additions of the input yield progressively smaller output or result in diminishing increases in output. The basic premise is that more is not always better. Likewise in healthcare, when providing value for the patients, it is imperative to keep all variables in the COS-Q in balance. Hence, with the value proposition, less can be more.

In an optimized model, there needs to be a balance between quality, service, operations, and finance. For example, when measuring the ALOS, it is imperative to optimize the patient's stay to provide the best financial results without sacrificing quality, service, or operational resources. Retrospectively, if the ALOS is "maximized" for the best financial results, the readmit rates may become higher and/or patient complaints may increase with degradation in both service and quality.

Chapter 3

New Metrics for Success

Errors using inadequate data are much less than those using no data at all.

Charles Babbage

In this chapter, readers will learn:

- limitations of existing discharge planning metrics
- the alignment of discharge planning data with hospital data
- the elements of a Core Measure scorecard

Traditional measures in discharge planning often include measuring staff productivity ratios, average length of stay (ALOS), payer mix, readmission rates, denial rate, and appeal rates. This data set, although important, is a very limited selection of what is actually required to manage a fully integrated discharge planning department. If information is power, then certainly having the right information to base decisions on is an indicator of future success.

Discharge planning data is especially difficult to collect, compile, and analyze. Team members are inundated with day-to-day tasks and often perceive the task of collecting management data as a low priority. In the past, hospitals may have utilized audit tools and metrics that did not provide enough meaningful information, therefore the collection and reporting of data became a low priority and, ultimately, unimportant.

Aside from tracking departmental data as noted in Chapter 2, discharge planning departments must also be aware of hospital data that

Table 3.1 Expanded Metrics

Inflow/Admission Data	Medical-Necessity Data
Admission trends Emergency-center diversion rate Emergency-center hold times Post-anesthesia recovery-room holds Direct admit and transfer delays	Days meeting medical necessity (%) Days not meeting medical necessity (%) Concurrent denial rate Observation conversions Observation >24 h Days saved
Length-of-Stay Data	Discharge Data
Average length of stay (ALOS) ALOS by day of admit ALOS by discharge code Bed turnover rate	Discharge trends Average length of discharge Discharge delays Discharge-delay reasons Cancelled discharge
Variance or Delay Data	Denial and Appeal Data
Variance days Variance reason	Cases denied for medical necessity (%) Case overturned (%) Dollars per denied case
Customer Satisfaction	Readmit Rates
Initial discharge planning assessment completion time Patient satisfaction Physician satisfaction	Readmitted in 30 days (%) Readmitted in 7 days (%) Readmitted within 24 h of discharge (%) Readmit reason
Referral Data	Quality Data
Referral tracking Referral reason	Core Measure compliance

is related to the discharge planning function. Grouping these metrics into structured categories allows information to be linked in ways that can provide a meaningful summary to the end-user. For example, if medical necessity is not being managed appropriately, the ALOS (a core discharge planning metric) will increase. This in turn may force hospitals operating at a high census to initiate emergency department (ED) diversions (a hospital-based capacity metric). Both events are interconnected and must be evaluated in tandem. Table 3.1 provides a summary of important metrics that span the elements of discharge planning across the entire acute-care continuum.

Expanded Metrics

Inflow/Admission Data

Most hospitals experience the battle of demand versus capacity on a daily basis. At some point, this tends to balance itself during the evening shift, and, if not then, it does balance by the end of the week. During moments of high census, an extreme amount of pressure is placed on hospital resources, as well as the patients and family members involved. Often termed as demand flow, it is one of the most critical values to understand when attempting to troubleshoot patient throughput and the relationship to discharge planning. Table 3.2 provides common data elements that should be collected and grouped together for review. This allows forward-thinking organizations to determine the impact of discharge planning on demand flow.

Length-of-Stay Data

Once the patient enters the system, there are a number of data elements that should be tracked in an effort to understand hidden bottlenecks during the patient's episode of care. The discharge planning department must understand its role in supporting patient *throughput* (See Table 3.3.) When the data sets are viewed in this fashion, team members are able to understand the relationship of the ALOS, and how ALOS can be impacted by day of admission or by discharge type.

Variance Data

Table 3.4 provides information about the reasons for variances in a patient's hospital stay. Common variances included delayed test results, failure to order necessary tests, and delayed or cancelled tests. Each variance typically increases the ALOS by 12 to 24 hours. This results not only in sluggish turnover and frustrated patients, family members, and physicians, but also creates unnecessary cost.

Medical-Necessity Data

Medical necessity data is often the most difficult to track and review. This information highlights cases that may be occupying an acute-care bed and may not have enough clinical criteria to secure appropriate reimbursement

Table 3.2 Inflow/Admission Data

Data Element	Definition	Track by	Significance
Admission trends	Patterns at which patients are registered as an observation or inpatient into the facility Patterns at which admissions occur	Hour of the day Days of the week	Understand peak flow Can potentially highlight patient throughput bottlenecks May be used to prioritize cancellation decisions
Emergency-center diversion rate	Time when ambulances are redirected from one hospital emergency room to another Total number of hours diverted divided by total hours of service	Per hour Per day Per month Per year	Forms baseline metrics Assists with identifying problem areas such as door to doctor time, lab and diagnostic turnaround times, and hospital capacity issues
Emergency-center hold time	Amount of time a patient waits in the emergency center for bed placement into the hospital Time starts when a physician order is obtained to register the patient as an observation or inpatient, and ends when the patient has been transferred to the room	Hour of the day Day of the week	Highlights hospital bottlenecks and internal bed turnover issues that can potentially be smoothed out by effective discharge planning
Postanesthesia care unit (PACU) holds	The number of cases that are held in PACU above target time due to no transfer bed	Hour of the day Day of the week	Helps identify financial resources lost due to internal hospital demand flow/discharges
Direct admit and transfer delays or cancellations	Number of direct admits or transfers requesting to be registered into the hospitals that are delayed or cancelled due to high volume Number of cancellations and delays divided by total requests	Hour of the day Day of the week Per month Per year	Helps identify financial resources lost due to internal hospital demand flow/discharge

Table 3.3 Length of Stay Data

Data Element	Definition	Track by	Significance
ALOS	Average amount of time a patient stays in a hospital Can be identified by diagnosis, unit, or overall number of total days in the hospital divided by total cases	Diagnosis Overall ALOS Diagnosis and physician	Helps identify high-level throughput data and should be used for comparison data
ALOS based on day of admit	Average amount of time a patient stays in a hospital based on the specific day of the admission	Calculating the ALOS as it relates to admit day (i.e., Monday vs. Tuesday) (Need to establish baseline)	Helps identify data triggers associated with throughput management based on specific day
ALOS for patients that require post-acute-care needs	Average amount of time a patient stays in a hospital based on the discharge status code admission	ALOS based on discharge code	Helps identify potential discharge planning bottlenecks
Bed turnover rate	Total number of patients using one bed in the span of a year Number of patients admitted to beds over a period of time	Best if tracked globally and then by bed type	Helps organization measure the impact of slow turn rates on revenue

for the stay. According to MPRO, the Medicare quality improvement organization for Michigan, one-fifth of 1,959 acute-care hospital admissions for 17 diagnosis-related groups (DRGs) lacked medical necessity.[1] Depending on the type of health plan, this could result in huge losses for the organization. For example, if the health plan reimburses by DRGs, reimbursement is capped off at a set amount. If the patient does not meet medical necessity, the hospital is basically spending down potential revenue. At times, there are outlier payments awarded; however, these do not typically cover the cost of the stay.

Many times a health plan may deny the stay while the patient is still in the hospital. It is important for hospitals to aggressively address these

Table 3.4   Variance Data

Data Element	Definition	Track by	Significance
Variance days	Department or service that causes a 24-h delay in patient treatment or plan of care decision	Per month Per year	Helps identify high-level throughput data and should be used for process improvement and comparison data
Variance reason	Reason for the variance (medical, transportation, test delay)	Reasons per month Reasons per year (Need to establish baseline)	Helps identify data triggers associated with throughput management for various hospital functions during an episode of care

denials concurrently and attempt to facilitate physician to physician inter-action conversations. It is easier to overturn a denial concurrently.

Failure to manage cases that are registered in observation status is costly. Hospitals must understand the payer rules around observations and how observation cases are reimbursed. Additionally, a process for billing these observation charges must be implemented. In one 700+ bed hospital, utili-zation-review team members worked alongside the billing-department team to assist with the concurrent collection of the documentation required to bill ancillary charges. The hospital recovered over $1.2 million in ancillary charges during the first year of implementation.

Days saved are days that would have been variance days had the mem-bers of the discharge planning team not intervened. Obtaining this data allows the department to demonstrate the value that it brings to the hospital. It is estimated that each day saved reduces costs by $300/day. This is a very conservative number and does not include dollars gained by increasing bed turnover rates.

Each data set in this grouping has a direct correlation with costs, and when this aspect is not managed effectively, costs increase and margins shrink. Hospitals can no longer tolerate the inability of discharge planning departments to understand and take action on measures to control cost and secure revenue.

Discharge Data

Analyzing the discharge data helps team members identify hidden opportunities to improve the actual discharge planning process. These improvements can lead to rapid bed turnover, improved patient and physician satisfaction, and better coordination of the throughput process. It is estimated that 30% of all discharges require more-complex discharge planning. Conversely, 70% of the time, the discharge planning process should be well controlled and expedited. The data set noted in Table 3.6 assists with identifying potential trouble areas.

Denial-and-Appeal Data

In many businesses, the most expensive table or seat is the empty one. In the healthcare industry, the most expensive bed is not the empty bed; rather, it is the occupied bed that is not getting reimbursed and is blocking a successful bed turn. Therefore, bed turnover rates and denial-and-appeal tracking and trending are other significant values to review. The data in Table 3.7 list common data elements that, when tracked and analyzed, can assist hospitals in identifying target areas for improvement.

Readmit Data

One of the most difficult metrics to assess is the actual strength of the discharge planning process. One data set that can provide some information is the review and evaluation of hospital readmit rates. This data set can be controversial, as readmit rates are poorly understood and ill-defined. Despite the ambiguity, readmit rates are becoming increasingly recognized as a useful metric. Hospital admission and readmission rates have increased over the last few decades.[2] It is estimated that repeated admissions might be responsible for up to 60% of hospital expenditure.[2] There are significant economic concerns related to readmission rates. Additionally, other studies relate readmission data as a measure of the quality of care delivered in a hospital. It is claimed that a significant number of readmissions are avoidable and potentially preventable.[2]

Published data regarding hospital readmissions demonstrate a wide variation in rates and patterns. This is in part due to a lack of uniformity in measures and definitions, and whether or not the readmission was planned

Table 3.5 Medical-Necessity Data

Data Element	Definition	Tracking	Significance
Days meeting medical necessity (%)	Total days that meet medical necessity divided by total patient days	Per month Annual trend line	Helps identify the strength of the utilization review process
Days not meeting medical necessity (%)	Total days that did not meet medical necessity divided by total patient days	Per month Annual trend line	Helps identify the strength of the utilization review process
Concurrent denial rate	Total concurrent days denied divided by total patient days	Per month Annual trend line	Helps identify concurrent medical necessity issues; allows for process to be put in place before denials actually occur
Observation conversions	Total number of cases that are converted based on payer request	Inpatient-to-observation conversions by month and by year Observation-to-inpatient conversions by month and by year Also track by health plan and physician	Helps identify payers that are converting; highlights cases for review and challenge May identify physician or physician groups who do not understand use of observation
Observation cases >24 h	Total number of cases that remain in observation status greater than 24 h	Total cases by month and year May consider tracking total days in excess of 24 h	Helps identify cases that may not be getting reimbursed and the strength of the utilization review process
Days saved	Total numbers of variance days minimized by the actions of a team member that results in increasing throughput	Per month Per year	Helps identify value of discharge planning/ care-coordination/ case-management oversight

Table 3.6   Discharge Data

Element	Definition	Track by	Significance
Discharge trend	Pattern at which patients are discharged from the hospital Patterns at which discharges occur	Discharges by hour Discharges by hour and by day of the week	Helps identify the discharge planning trends
Average length of discharge (ALOD)	Time required to transition a patient from hospital to next level of care Begins when the physician order is written for discharge and ends when the patient has exited the facility	Auditing time of discharge with actual time patient exits the facility	Helps identify the discharge delays
Discharge delay	Trend at which discharge delay occurs	Occurrences per week Occurrences per month Occurrences per year	Helps identify common delays that occur at the point of discharge
Discharge delay reason	Actual reason for discharge delay	Reason by month Reason by year	Helps identify discharge delay reasons and trends
Cancelled discharge reasons	Reason and frequency of cancelled discharges	Per month Per year	Helps identify the reason discharges cancel

or unplanned. Further, patients may not readmit to the same hospital, further exacerbating the difficulty of data collection and analysis.

For example, a patient presents on a Friday with chest pain. The patient has a cardiac catheterization that demonstrates blockages, which will require a coronary artery bypass. The patient's chest pain is under control and there is no evidence of infarct. The blockages are not emergent, and the physician has determined that the patient can be discharged with plans to perform the surgery the following Monday. The patient is discharged for the weekend to spend time with family members prior to surgery. The physician writes orders to discharge the patient and writes specific orders in the event pain

Table 3.7   Denial-and-Appeal Data

Data Element	Definition	Track by	Significance
Cases denied for medical necessity (%)	Total number of patient cases that are denied for medical necessity divided by total cases	Per month Per year	Helps measure the strength of the utilization-review function
Cases overturned (%)	Total number of cases successfully appealed divided by total cases denied	Per month Per year	Helps measure the strength of the utilization-review function
Average denied dollar per case	Total denied dollars divided by total number of denied cases	Per month Per year	Helps companies measure the impact of a denied claim
Total denied days	Total days denied by health plan	Per month Per year	Helps identify potential capacity

would return. The patient subsequently readmits the following Monday for surgery. This example would trigger a readmit. If readmit data is not closely evaluated, this could seem unfavorable. However, in this case, the patient has a health plan that reimburses on a DRG system, thereby reducing the ALOS by two days (Saturday and Sunday), reducing costs. In this case, the patient needs were met, and the cost, operations, service, and quality of care (COS-Q) was optimized.

There are wide variations in published readmit data. Overall, the readmission rates in the adult population vary from 5% to 29%.[2] It has been proposed that the increased readmission rates are perhaps the inevitable price of early discharge.[2] Although a premature discharge can be an important factor, a positive correlation between the two has not been identified. Several studies have attempted to identify ways to prevent readmission from occurring. The strategies employed include improved hospital inpatient care, robust discharge planning, increased access to outpatient services, and improved community support or a combination of these measures.[2] One study examined the role of a nurse-led multidisciplinary intervention in preventing the readmission of elderly patients with heart failure. The study demonstrated a reduction in the rate of readmission, an improvement in the quality of care, and a decrease in the overall cost of medical care over a period of three months.[2]

Table 3.8   Readmit Rates

Data Element	Definition	Track by	Significance
Cases readmitted in 30 days or 7 days or within 24 h of discharge (%)	Total number of cases that discharged divided by total number of cases that readmitted Can be tracked by period of time (30 days, 7 days, or within 24 h) or by diagnosis of physician	Per indicator per month Per indicator per year	Helps measure the strength of the discharge plan; also helps identify areas for improvement Has some financial indicators
Readmit reason	Reason the patient was readmitted	Per month Per year	Identifies reason for readmits

In view of the cost and quality implication of readmissions, members of the discharge planning team must attempt to understand and implement strategies to prevent the likelihood of unplanned readmissions. These measures result in improved cost savings, optimized operations (through better resource utilization), improved customer service, and improved quality (COS-Q).

In the aforementioned example, the discharge planner should recognize that allowing the patient to go home brings balance to the COS-Q equation. Costs are minimized by two days; proper communication to the patient, physician, family, and team members improves operations; service to the customer is favorable; and the quality of care is enhanced.

Table 3.8 defines three common types of readmit data that can be collected. Consider tracking and analyzing readmits that occur within 24 hours, 7 days, and 30 days of discharge. If the reason for the readmit can also be determined, discharge planning team members can implement readmit-reduction strategies.

Customer Service Data

As hospitals position for quality and transparency, customer service and the customer value proposition will become increasingly significant. Wikipedia defines customer service as "the provision of service before, during and after a purchase." As hospitals position for consumerism, customer service will become a significant competitive advantage. Further, the customer value proposition, or perceived value to the customer for services rendered, should also be evaluated. As noted in earlier chapters, the consistent delivery of

Table 3.9   Customer Service Data

Data Element	Definition	Track by	Significance
Initial discharge planning assessment completion time	Time it takes to complete the initial discharge planning assessment; begins when patient is admitted; ends when form assessment is completed	Admission time to unit until initial discharge planning assessment is completed	Helps identify potential discharge planning delays
Patient satisfaction	A survey used to identify the patient's perception of the discharge planning process	Developing discharge planning customer satisfaction surveys: • per month • per quarter • per year	Helps identify areas for improvement
Physician satisfaction	A survey used to identify the physician's perception of the discharge planning process	Developing discharge planning customer satisfaction surveys	Helps improve the physician perception of the discharge planning function

superior service requires the careful design and execution of a whole system of activities that includes people, processes, and technology. When executed successfully, the end result is an improved COS-Q.

Many hospitals attempt to gather information from patients through customer service surveys. Table 3.9 identifies customer service data elements that should be tracked. Special attention must be given to the survey questions. Queries must be reflective and written in a way that will assist members of the discharge planning team to hone in on issues and rapidly design strategies for improvement.

Referral Data

Members of the discharge planning team interface with almost every physician, family member, and patient. Few of the discharge planners are aware of all the services that a hospital can provide its consumer. An integrated delivery system (IDS) is a network of healthcare providers and organizations that provides or arranges to provide a coordinated continuum of services to a defined population and is willing to be held clinically and fiscally accountable for the clinical outcomes and health status of the population served.[3] An IDS may own or could be closely aligned with an insurance product. Services provided by an IDS can include a fully-equipped community and/or tertiary hospital, home healthcare and hospice services, primary and specialty outpatient care and surgery, social services, rehabilitation, preventive care, health education, and financing, usually using a form of managed care. An IDS can also be a training location for health-professional students, including physicians, nurses, and allied health professionals.

As a member of a discharge planning team, it is important to be aware of services that can be coordinated for a patient. For example, a member of the discharge planning team may be coordinating services for a newly diagnosed diabetic patient. As an advocate of care, it makes sense that a discharge planner would discuss the opportunity to obtain an order for diabetic education from the physician. The patient can choose to go to any diabetic education center, but may not have knowledge of the resources available. Discharge planners must be able to provide the patient with contact information for local services, and should be prepared to discuss the option of receiving service within the IDS. The outcome for a patient is improved education in a comfortable setting, improved quality of care, and potentially a reduction in hospital readmissions related to diabetic complications.

As consumerism begins to dominate the healthcare sector, becoming the consumer's provider of choice is vital. Members of the discharge planning team serve as a direct gateway to the consumer; they have an ability to communicate services and track and understand what services a consumer should and would choose (See Table 3.10).

Quality Data

Hospitals are struggling with managing the significant volume of human capital required to meet accreditation and public reporting requirements. Core Measures track evidence-based, scientifically researched standards of care, which have been shown to result in improved clinical outcomes for patients. CMS (Centers for Medicare & Medicaid Services) established the Core Measures in 2000 and began publicly reporting data relating to the

Table 3.10   Referral Data

Data Element	Definition	Track by	Significance
Referral tracking	Number of post-acute care referrals that are secured internally divided by total referrals	Referrals per month Referrals per year	Helps identify opportunities to become the consumer's provider of choice
Referral reason	Reasons consumers chose a particular provider	Per month Per year	Helps companies understand the driver for patient choice

Core Measures in 2003. Currently, there are 26 Core Measures spread over four areas: Heart Failure (HF), Acute Myocardial Infarction (AMI), Pneumonia (CAP), and Surgical Care Improvement Project (SCIP). These are depicted in Tables 3.11–3.14.

Hospital reimbursement and quality of patient care require hospitals to manage data submission for public inspection. Meeting the compliance standards requires effectively obtaining physician orders or required documentation, and then collecting and reporting the information. The tracking and reporting of Core Measure performance is an enormous amount of work that occupies a team of clinical members. There is no funding to support the cost of tracing and reporting of the data; therefore hospitals must find solutions to meeting the mandate while managing the costs. It is anticipated that the number of Core Measures will expand dramatically, thus increasing the workload and costs associated with supporting the mandate.

In an independent study of the data collection effort, one of the participating measurement systems (the Qualidigm Quality Partnership) measured time spent abstracting data per case for 10 Rhode Island hospitals. Each hospital collected data for three Core Measure sets (AMI, HF, and CAP) for a period of 12 months. After analysis and review, the results[4] were as follows:

AMI = 27 min (0.45 h/case)

HF = 22.2 min (0.37 h/case)

CAP = 23.4 min (0.39 h/case)

Hospitals can estimate the amount of resources required per measurement by multiplying the median abstraction time per case. This amount can

Table 3.11 Core Measure Data: Acute Myocardial Infarction (AMI)

Code	Indicator	Definition
AMI-1	Aspirin at arrival	AMI patients without aspirin contraindications who received aspirin within 24 h before or after hospital arrival
AMI-2	Aspirin prescribed at discharge	AMI patients without aspirin contraindications who are prescribed aspirin at hospital discharge
AMI-3	ACEI or ARB for LVSD	AMI patients with left ventricular systolic dysfunction (LVSD) and without both angiotensin-converting enzyme inhibitor (ACEI) and angiotensin receptor blocker (ARB) contraindications who are prescribed an ACEI or ARB at hospital discharge
AMI-4	Adult smoking-cessation advice/ counseling	AMI patients with a history of smoking cigarettes who are given smoking-cessation advice or counseling during hospital stay (For purposes of this measure, a smoker is defined as someone who has smoked cigarettes anytime during the year prior to hospital arrival.)
AMI-5	Beta blocker prescribed at discharge	AMI patients without beta blocker contraindications who are prescribed a beta blocker at hospital discharge
AMI-6	Beta blocker at arrival	AMI patients without beta blocker contraindications who received a beta blocker within 24 h after hospital arrival
AMI-7	Median time to thrombolysis	Median time from arrival to administration of a thrombolytic agent in patients with ST segment elevation or left-bundle branch block (LBBB) on the electrocardiogram (ECG) performed closest to hospital arrival time
AMI-7a	Thrombolytic agent received within 30 min of hospital arrival	AMI patients receiving thrombolytic therapy during the hospital stay and having a time from hospital arrival to thrombolysis of 30 min or less
AMI-8	Median time to PTCA	Median time from arrival to percutaneous transluminal coronary angioplasty (PTCA) in patients with ST segment elevation or LBBB on the ECG performed closest to hospital arrival time

(continued)

Table 3.11 (continued)   Core Measure Data: Acute Myocardial Infarction (AMI)

Code	Indicator	Definition
AMI-8a	PCI received within 90 min of hospital arrival	AMI patients receiving primary percutaneous coronary intervention (PCI) during the hospital stay with a time from hospital arrival to PCI of 90 min or less
AMI-9	The Joint Commission on the Accreditation of Health Care Organizations (JCAHO) only inpatient mortality	AMI patients who expire during hospital stay

Table 3.12   Core Measure Data: Heart Failure (HF)

Code	Indicator	Definition
HF-1	Discharge instructions	Heart failure patients discharged home with written discharge instructions or educational material given to patient or caregiver at discharge or during the hospital stay addressing all of the following: activity level, diet, discharge medications, follow-up appointment, weight monitoring, and information on what to do if symptoms worsen
HF-2	Left ventricular function (LVF) assessment	Heart failure patients with documentation in the hospital record that LVF was assessed before arrival, during hospitalization, or is planned after discharge
HF-3	ACEI or ARB for LVSD	Heart failure patients with LVSD and without both ACEI and ARB contraindications who are prescribed an ACEI or ARB at hospital discharge (For purposes of this measure, LVSD is defined as chart documentation of a Left Ventricular Ejection Fraction [LVEF] less than 40% or a narrative description of LVF consistent with moderate or severe systolic dysfunction.)
HF-4	Adult smoking-cessation advice/ counseling	Heart failure patients with a history of smoking cigarettes who are given smoking-cessation advice or counseling during hospital stay (For purposes of this measure, a smoker is defined as someone who has smoked cigarettes anytime during the year prior to hospital arrival.)

Table 3.13   Core Measure Data: Pneumonia (PN)

Code	Indicator	Definition
PN-1	Oxygenation assessment	Pneumonia (PN) patients who had an assessment of arterial oxygenation by arterial blood gas measurement or pulse oximetry within 24 h prior to or after arrival at the hospital
PN-2	Pneumococcal screening and/or vaccination	Pneumonia patients age 65 and older who were screened for pneumococcal vaccine status and were administered the vaccine prior to discharge, if indicated
PN-3a	Blood cultures performed within 24 h prior to or 24 h after hospital arrival for patients who were transferred or admitted to the Intensive Care Unit (ICU) within 24 h of hospital arrival	Pneumonia patients transferred or admitted to the ICU within 24 h of hospital arrival, who had blood cultures performed within 24 h prior to or 24 h after hospital arrival
PN-3b	Blood cultures performed in the emergency department prior to initial antibiotic received in hospital	Pneumonia patients whose initial emergency room blood culture specimen was collected prior to first hospital dose of antibiotics
PN-4	Adult smoking cessation advice/counseling	Pneumonia patients with a history of smoking cigarettes who are given smoking cessation advice or counseling during hospital stay
PN-5	Antibiotic timing	The time, in minutes, from hospital arrival to administration of first antibiotic for inpatients with pneumonia
PN-5a	Initial antibiotic received within 8 h of hospital arrival	Pneumonia patients who receive their first dose of antibiotics within 8 h after arrival at the hospital
PN-5b	Initial antibiotic received within 4 h of hospital arrival	Pneumonia patients who receive their first dose of antibiotics within 4 h after arrival at the hospital
PN-6	Immunocompetent patients with community-acquired pneumonia (CAP)	Patients who receive an initial antibiotic regimen during the first 24 h that is consistent with current guidelines

(continued)

Table 3.13 (continued)   Core Measure Data: Pneumonia (PN)

Code	Indicator	Definition
PN-6a	Immunocompetent ICU patients with CAP who receive an initial antibiotic regimen during the first 24 h that is consistent with current guidelines	Immunocompetent patients for both ICU (PN-6a) and non-ICU (PN-6b) with pneumonia who receive an initial antibiotic regimen during the first 24 h that is consistent with current guidelines
PN-6b	Immunocompetent non-ICU patients with CAP who receive an initial antibiotic regimen during the first 24 h that is consistent with current guidelines	Immunocompetent patients for both ICU (PN-6a) and non-ICU (PN-6b) with pneumonia who receive an initial antibiotic regimen during the first 24 h that is consistent with current guidelines
PN-7	Influenza vaccination	Pneumonia patients age 50 years and older, hospitalized during October, November, December, January, or February, who were screened for influenza vaccine status and were vaccinated prior to discharge, if indicated

then be multiplied by the median rate of pay. This estimate only calculates the actual abstraction time and does not include calculations for physician interaction, concurrent overview, and patient education.

Undoubtedly, Core Measure performance is a data element that must be evaluated. Tables 3.11–3.14 denote Core Measure compliance. This is often evaluated using a quality "dashboard" or report card. As noted, the labor required to monitor and address Core Measure compliance is enormous, and hospitals are looking for opportunities to meet the mandate and leverage costs associated with this task. Many discharge planning departments include care-coordination registered nurses (RNs) or nursing members. Those that include a nursing component may want to consider utilizing the clinical nursing expertise to assist with identifying Core Measure compliance issues.

Traditional indicators are no longer valid in assessing the success of current discharge planning functions. As market forces continue to impact the healthcare industry, metrics will continue to evolve over time. Having the right systems and processes in place will ensure that management will have the right information to manage the function.

Table 3.14   Core Measure Data: Surgical Care Improvement Project (SCIP), Surgical Infection Prevention

Code	Indicator	Definition
SCIP- Inf-1 S	Prophylactic antibiotic received within 1 h prior to surgical incision	Surgical patients who received prophylactic antibiotics within 1 h prior to surgical incision (Patients who received vancomycin or a fluoroquinolone for prophylactic antibiotics should have the antibiotics administered within 2 h prior to surgical incision. Due to the longer infusion time required for vancomycin or a fluoroquinolone, it is acceptable to start these antibiotics within 2 h prior to incision time.)
SCIP- Inf-2	Prophylactic antibiotic selection for surgical patients	Surgical patients who received prophylactic antibiotics consistent with current guidelines (specific to each type of surgical procedure)
SCIP- Inf-3	Prophylactic antibiotics discontinued within 24 h after surgery end time	Surgical patients whose prophylactic antibiotics were discontinued within 24 h after surgery end time
SCIP- Inf-4	Cardiac surgery patients with controlled 6 a.m. postoperative serum glucose	Cardiac surgery patients with controlled 6 a.m. serum glucose (200 mg/dL) on postoperative day one (POD 1) and postoperative day two (POD 2), with Surgery End Date being postoperative day zero (POD 0)
SCIP- Inf-6	Surgery patients with appropriate hair removal	Surgery patients with appropriate surgical site hair removal. No hair removal, or hair removal with clippers or depilatory, is considered appropriate. Shaving is considered inappropriate.
SCIP- Inf-7	Colorectal surgery patients with immediate postoperative normothermia	Colorectal surgery patients with immediate normothermia (96.8°F –100.4°F) within the first hour after leaving the operating room

Aligning the department with enterprise-wide indicators is the key to assessing the COS-Q. For example, it is critical for the discharge planner to know if the organization is on diversions and the impact of that status on the department's operations. Additionally, it is critical to make it a priority to collect, compile, and analyze the information so that the process can be managed. Converting data into actionable intelligence will provide significant decision-support value, and therefore the process will reinforce itself as a priority among staff and management by default.

References

1. N. Youngstrom, "Admission Medical-Necessity Errors Abound: Hospitals Try New Compliance Strategies," *Report on Medicare Compliance* 14, no. 10 (March 21, 2005); http://www.lhcr.org/PDF/HPMPWorkBook/AppU_ReportMedicareCompliance.pdf.
2. M. Hasan, "Readmission of Patients to Hospital: Still Ill-defined and Poorly Understood," *Int. J. Qual. Health Care* 13, no. 3 (2001): 177–179; http://intqhc.oxfordjournals.org/cgi/reprint/13/3/177.pdf.
3. Washington State Hospital Association, "Integrated Delivery Systems," in *Governing Board Orientation Manual*, chap. 11. http://www.wsha.org/files/62/Gov_Bd_Manual_INTEGRATED.doc.
4. Joint Commission, www.jointcommission.org/Performancemeasures.

Chapter 4

Uncovering the Data Story

Information is the oxygen of the modern age.

Ronald Reagan

In this chapter, readers will learn:

- how to group data to tell the discharge planning "story"
- how to create the discharge planning snapshot

Based on the complexity of the discharge planning functions, management is often inundated with issues that consistently reemerge. Although solutions are developed to solve these issues, it is often only the symptoms that are being addressed. These symptoms are often evidence of underlying issues that, unless resolved, will not eliminate the problems. Hence, multiple indicators from various categories are often required to paint the right picture in order to identify the correct solutions. For example, Emergency Department (ED) diversions may mean that there are not enough beds, or that diagnostic turnaround times may be slow, or that the discharge planning process may be behind target.

Knowing which elements to "string together" is key to painting the right picture to root out the problems. Hospitals that successfully convert multiple data sets into actionable intelligence can quickly implement strategies for change. The following steps will take readers through a data analysis process that will highlight the role of the discharge planning department and its relationship to driving hospital outcomes or COS-Q (cost, operations, service, and quality of care).

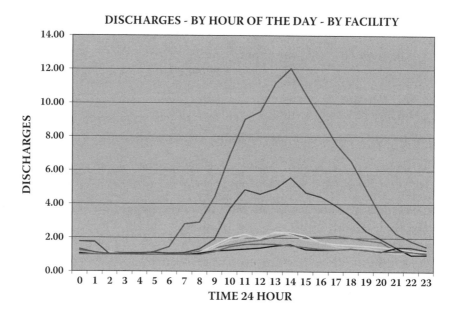

DISCHARGES - BY HOUR OF THE DAY - BY FACILITY

Figure 4.1   Sample discharge by hour of the day, six different hospitals

Inflow/Outflow Assessment

Step 1: Discharge Data

Begin by evaluating the discharge data. An hour-by-hour discharge trend line can help determine when peak discharge volumes occur. It is critical to understand operational processes when evaluating the data. Some units may enter all discharges into the ADT (admissions/discharges/transfers) system at a specific time of day. When data is entered in a batch formation, it can skew the data.

Figure 4.1 is an example of six different facilities that all seem to have very similar trend lines. Discharges begin around 11 a.m., with a noted peak around 2 p.m. and a drop-off around 9 p.m.

Step 2: Admission Data

Next, review the admission data. Notice the peak admission times. How they correspond to ED peaks? How they correspond to elective admissions and surgical admits? In a recent hospital evaluation, it was discovered that there were two distinct peaks, one between the hours of 6–8 a.m. and another in the 4–6 p.m. time period (see Figure 4.2).

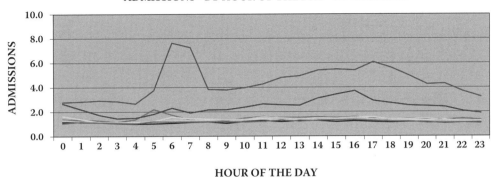

Figure 4.2   Sample admission data by hour of the day, eight different hospitals

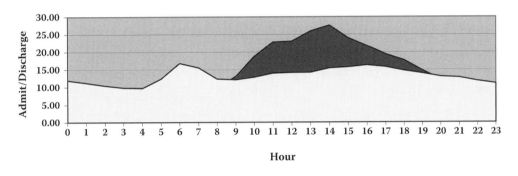

Figure 4.3   Sample combined discharge/admit data by hour of the day, six different hospitals

Step 3: The Relationship of the Admit and Discharge Data

Figure 4.1 and Figure 4.2 demonstrate the peaks and valleys of throughput. However, when you combine both figures, it becomes evident that there are specific areas that can be assessed to smooth out these variances (see Figure 4.3). The combined figure demonstrates that there is a potential opportunity to smooth the throughput process by building processes to impact the discharge planning time. Moving up the discharge time by one or two hours can improve operations and therefore improve cash flow.

Step 4: Look at Other Related Data

There are other data elements to consider, for instance linking admit and discharge data with ED diversions or ED holds. When admissions are at a peak and discharges are not, capacity is strained. When capacity is at its maximum, the impact on operations can be costly. This exercise can quickly demonstrate bottlenecks that need to be addressed.

Throughput Management Assessment

Step 1: Length-of-Stay Data

Average length of stay (ALOS) is another important data element to track. However, the data can be misleading when the calculation of the data is not understood. For instance, a hospital may average a one-day surgical stay and nine-day medical stay, thus the ALOS is five days. Initially, this might look favorable. However, if a patient has a nine-day medical stay and is only meeting criteria for the first four days, the hospital will lose reimbursement. Expanding the data to look at "linked" data sets can provide hospitals with more meaningful ways to calculate ALOS. Discharge planning team members must also determine how ALOS impacts hospital reimbursement. Hospitals that have favorable ALOS data may consider analyzing more stratified data subsets, which include ALOS by payer, DRG (diagnosis-related group), or case type.

Step 2: Relationship Between Day of Admission and Length-of-Stay Data

What is the impact of the day of admission on the ALOS? If a patient was admitted on Monday, how does this impact the length of stay compared with an admit on Friday? Figure 4.4 is a graphic representation of seven sample hospitals and the ALOS based on the patient's day of admission. The data suggests the longest length of stay occurs when patients are admitted on Mondays and Fridays. What happens on Mondays and Fridays?

In some hospitals, a vast majority of major surgical cases are admitted on Monday. Therefore, it may not be a significant variance. In the sample hospitals, it was noted that when admissions occurred on Friday, the ALOS increased. Further review demonstrated that in these seven facilities, many departments "closed" on Saturdays and Sundays, only responding to stat or emergency needs. These departments are typically gastrointestinal, interventional radiology, ultrasound, and diagnostic cardiovascular catheterization departments. When these departments "close," there can be considerable

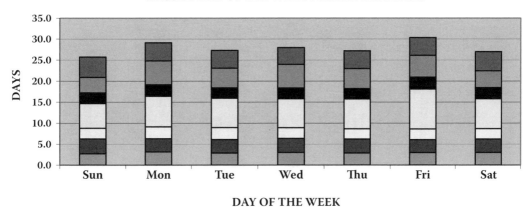

Figure 4.4   Average length of stay based on day of the admission

implications to ALOS, customer satisfaction, reimbursement, and hospital operations. When comparing this type of data, it is important to run the compare groups against each other: ED admits to ED admits, scheduled admits to scheduled admits, etc.

Step 3: Average Length of Stay for Patients Requiring Post-Acute Care

How does the length of stay for patients that require post-acute-care services compare? Many times there is an increased length of stay due to discharge planning delays. Figure 4.5 is a comparative schematic that demonstrates the ALOS for patients that required post-acute-care services. The diagram compares the ALOS for a specific discharge code against the same discharge type at five other hospitals. For example, patients that were assigned a discharge code that specified home-care services had an ALOS that ranged anywhere from one to eight days. Identifying the discharge codes and then comparing the ALOS assigned by code allowed this organization to focus on factors that could improve these outcomes. In Figure 4.5, seven hospitals are being compared. Note the variations between the facilities for other post-acute-care services.

Step 4: Bed Turnover Rate

When discharge planning is implemented appropriately, there should be a correlation to the bed turnover rate. While there are other variables that

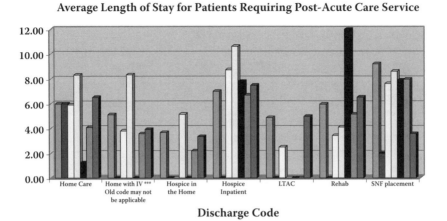

Figure 4.5   Average length of stay for patients requiring post-acute care

impact bed turnover rates, the discharge planning process and utilization-review process are two important drivers. Hospitals that have initiated processes designed to smooth out the discharge planning and utilization-review processes have significantly increased bed turnover rates and, in essence, released 5%–20% of hidden bed capacity.[1]

Step 5: Variance Data

Once a hospital is able to determine how different departments and/or hospital functions influence the ALOS, it is time to look further for specific reasons why there are delays in an episode of care. These delays are often referred to as *avoidable days* or *variance days* (days that could potentially be avoided). How many days are lost and why? Figure 4.6 is a representation of a facility's total number of variance days for the year. In this scenario, this facility identified over 3,000 days that resulted in a greater than one-day delay in care, services, or discharge. The ability to identify opportunities to minimize variances actually assists with capacity management.

In addition to recording the number of variances, it is important to record the reason that the variance occurred. Figure 4.7 is an example of hospital variance reasons that are typically recorded. Conservatively, this hospital assigned $300 in costs to every variance day, which equated to over $1 million in added costs. Variance days that are identified as preventable add costs and shrink margins when they are not addressed. Managing this data is critical to capacity management and COS-Q.

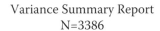

Variance Summary Report
N=3386

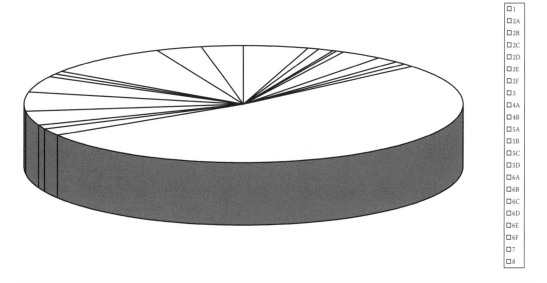

□1	
□2A	
□2B	
□2C	
□2D	
□2E	
□2F	
□3	
□4A	
□4B	
□5A	
□5B	
□5C	
□5D	
□6A	
□6B	
□6C	
□6D	
□6E	
□6F	
□7	
□8	

Figure 4.6   Variance summary report

Variance Reason	Variance Description
1	SW failed to see patient or initiate a timely D/C plan
2A	CARD/VASC/NEUR - hospital failure test/order not done on a timely basis
2B	RADIOLOGY/NUC MED - hospital failure test/order not done on a timely basis
2C	LAB/PATH - hospital failure test/order not done on a timely basis
2D	ENDO/GI - hospital failure test/order not done on a timely basis
2E	ANES/SCHED - hospital failure test/order not done on a timely basis
2F	OTHER - hospital failure test/order not done on a timely basis
3	Psych consult not obtained on a timely basis (one day)
4A	Spec. Consult not obtained on a timely basis (one day)
4B	Spec. Consult/treatment not completed (PT/OT/ST)
5A	Physician variance
5B	Staff Nurse variance
5C	Clinical Care Manager variance
5D	Patient/Family variance
6A	No SNF/ECF bed available
6B	No TCU bed available
6C	No REHAB bed available
6D	No HOSPICE bed available
6E	No HOME CARE available
6F	No TRANSFER BED available - Step-down, Med/Surg
7	Regulatory-IMM
8	Other - Add Comment

Figure 4.7   Variance code and variance code description

Step 6: Percentage of Days Meeting Medical Necessity/ Not Meeting Medical Necessity

The strength of the utilization-review process can be measured by auditing a patient's entire episode of care and determining the percentage of days that meet and do not meet medical necessity. During one assessment of a children's hospital, it became evident that, many times, an entire stay did not meet medical necessity. The end result was denial of payment. It is important to have a strong understanding of the barriers associated with facilitating the discharge of patients that are no longer meeting criteria for acute care. There are two ways to track this data. The first is to perform a retrospective review of an episode of care. This assists with determining what percentage of the admission met criteria and what percentage did not. The second way to measure this data is to concurrently obtain a count of how many cases in the hospital meet and do not meet medical necessity on a given day.

In the case of the children's hospital, the retrospective audits revealed that almost 70% of cases had portions of the stay that did not meet medical necessity. The concurrent audit revealed that approximately 33% of the patients on any given day did not meet medical necessity. This data suggests that there are great opportunities to expedite discharge, increase bed turnover, and release hidden capacity.

Step 7: Concurrent Denial Rates

Denials that are due to lack of medical necessity strongly correlate with the strength of the utilization-review and discharge planning functions. Analyzing the concurrent and retrospective denial data best evaluates this. The concurrent denial rate is the rate at which health plans are concurrently denying cases while the patient is still in the hospital. The retrospective denial rate is a medical-necessity denial that occurs after the patient has been discharged. Dollars denied per case represent the average dollars lost per case for denials. Instituting specific protocols for concurrent denials is vital. In some hospitals, there is a process for concurrent-denial reversals. This process includes the following:

- identification of concurrent denial
- communication to attending physician by members of the discharge planning department (utilization-review nurse)

- coordination of hospital physician to health-plan physician for concurrent appeal
- tracking of concurrent denial and outcome of concurrent appeal

It is also impetrative for hospitals to track the number of cases denied and, if at all possible, the number of days denied.

Step 8: Observation Conversion Rate Data

Tracking and monitoring observation conversion rates is another important aspect of understanding the discharge planning department. It has been suggested by some that a conversion request by a health plan from inpatient status to observation status is a buried denial. In other words, commercial payers may deny payment for a case concurrently unless the discharge planning team member changes the case status to observation. There are facilities that would rather convert a case to observation than take a denial on the back end of the process. However, if this information is tracked, there may be trends with particular payers who use this strategy to control costs. In one facility, a payer typically converted 90 cases per month; of the 90 cases, 95% were forced conversions from inpatient to observation status. Further, the decision to convert the case was often suggested 48 to 72 hours after the admission. Interestingly enough, when patients were in observation status, this payer contract only paid $150/day plus ancillary charges. After the first 24 hours in observation status, reimbursement stopped. After implementing process changes, the inpatient-to-observation conversion rate decreased to 55%.

Step 9: Observation >24 Hours

Discharge planning department members must be aware of observation cases. Cases that remain in the hospital for greater than 24 hours should be the exception, not the norm. Managing observation cases requires knowledge of payer reimbursement and CMS (Centers for Medicare and Medicaid Services) guidelines, and an understanding of how to bill for ancillary charges. Millions of dollars are lost in hospitals that fail to manage this patient population. Members of the discharge planning team, specifically the members responsible for utilization review, must understand how to impact these cases. This involves frequent communication with the patient, physician, and bedside nurses, as well as communication with the billing-team members.

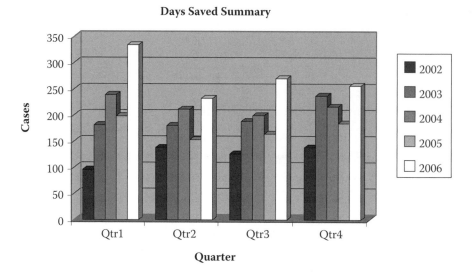

Figure 4.8   Days saved summary

Step 10: Days-Saved Data

Variance data can provide a summary of barriers or bottlenecks in day-to-day operations, while *days saved* (number of days that, if not "saved" or impacted, would result in a variance) reveals the number of days that were impacted by members of your discharge planning team. Figure 4.8 is a diagram of a facility that tracked days saved. Note the increase in days saved once the data was tracked and reviewed by members of the discharge planning team. Days saved results in minimizing costs and the release of hidden capacity.

Discharge Data Assessment

Step 1: Discharge Trends

Understanding peak discharge times helps hospitals position resources in a more effective manner. In one study, peak discharges occurred from 4 to 6 p.m. and gradually decelerated from 7 to 9 p.m. As discussed earlier in this chapter, moving the discharge time up by 1–2 hours per day can have a significant impact on inflow. The ability to capture a bed an hour earlier may reduce the number of cancelled surgeries or emergency center diversions.

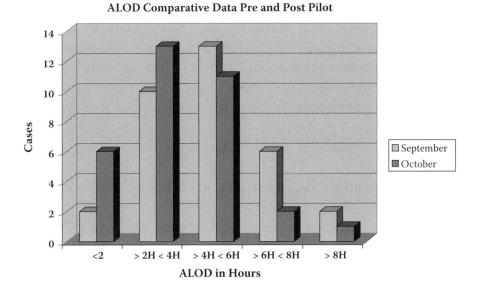

Figure 4.9 **Comparative chart of ALOD data for one hospital before and after implementation of Lean Six Sigma**

Step 2: Average Length of Discharge

The average length of discharge (ALOD) is determined by comparing the time a discharge order was written with the time the patient actually left the facility. During a pilot study conducted in a facility in 2006, the ALOD varied from 1 to 18 hours. There were a number of reasons that delays in the discharge occurred, and these reasons varied from unit to unit. Figure 4.9 represents a hospital's comparative data. The data compared the baseline ALOD with the ALOD after Lean–Six Sigma processes were implemented. During the pilot, ALOD time periods were grouped into the following categories:

- less than 2 hours
- 2–4 hours
- 4–6 hours
- 6–8 hours
- greater than 8 hours

The pilot study focused members of the discharge planning team on performing an initial discharge screen within the first 24 hours of

admission. The screen was conducted by a nurse who would further identify if there were clinical indications for post-acute-care needs. The nurse
would also identify any potential barriers to discharge. If the patient was
at risk for needing post-acute-care services or likely to have barriers to a
smooth discharge, this triggered a referral to the social work team member.
Once the social worker became involved, the patient was monitored on a
daily basis until discharge. At the conclusion of the pilot study, the ALOD
decreased by an average of 33 minutes per patient, as seen in Figure 4.9.

Step 3: Discharge Delay Reasons

Discharge delay reasons can be recorded as a variance, or they can be
targeted to specifically provide discharge delay data. Reasons for discharge
delays vary from unit to unit, and are due to different clinical and patient
care needs. The following is a list of common delay reasons:

- not medically cleared for discharge
- transportation issues
- family issues
- delayed test results
- waiting for skilled bed
- guardianship issues

Although not all delays can be controlled, there are a number of actions
members of the discharge planning team can take to reduce the total number of delay days. For instance, discussions about transportation barriers
should occur within 24 hours of admission. This gives both the patient and
the discharge planning team member time to coordinate plans. Family issues
can often be minimized when a key contact person is identified and care is
coordinated and communicated to those persons. Obtaining a skilled bed at
the time services are needed can be a struggle. However, when communication to the accepting facility occurs in a timely and consistent manner, delays
can be minimized. While not all delays can be averted, there are processes
that can be implemented to reduce their occurrence.

Step 4: Cancelled Discharges

At times, a patient's medical condition will change, resulting in cancellation
of an ordered discharge. One hospital noticed an increase in cancelled

discharges and attempted to identify the reasons why the increase was occurring. After careful review, members of the team identified an interesting finding—sometimes, patients would convince the bedside nurse to let them stay an additional evening. Further, the patient would appeal to the evening rounding physician, and the physician would hold the patient until the next day. It is important to note that the last 24 hours of a patient's episode of care is the time frame most vulnerable to payment denials. Managing the day before and the day of discharge is crucial.

Utilization Review Assessment

Step 1: Percentage of Cases Denied for Medical Necessity

The most important role of the discharge planning department (assuming that utilization review is part of that department) is to "defend" the reason a patient is receiving acute-care services. If team members are unable to uphold an acute-care stay, it is their primary function to interact with members of the healthcare team to facilitate a discharge. This involves communicating the clinical findings to a physician and attempting to help the physician and the bedside nurse understand why a discharge is required.

Under conditions of participation for the Centers for Medicare & Medicaid Services, discharge planning departments must act as gatekeepers for patients served under these programs. This practice is being increasingly regulated and audited for compliance. Failure to communicate information to the physician and patient can result in fines to the hospital and denial of payment. Keeping patients in the acute-care setting when the level of care is not justified is considered fraudulent practice. The strength of a discharge planning department and its ability to correctly apply standardized criteria should be valued.

Step 2: Average Dollars per Denied Case

Figure 4.10 is a depiction of average dollars denied per case in five different facilities. This figure shows a two-year review of the average amount of dollars denied per case. These denials were based on medical necessity. According to the data, there has been an increase in the average dollars denied per case. This could mean that more days are being denied, or it could mean that the utilization-review process has weakened. Understanding

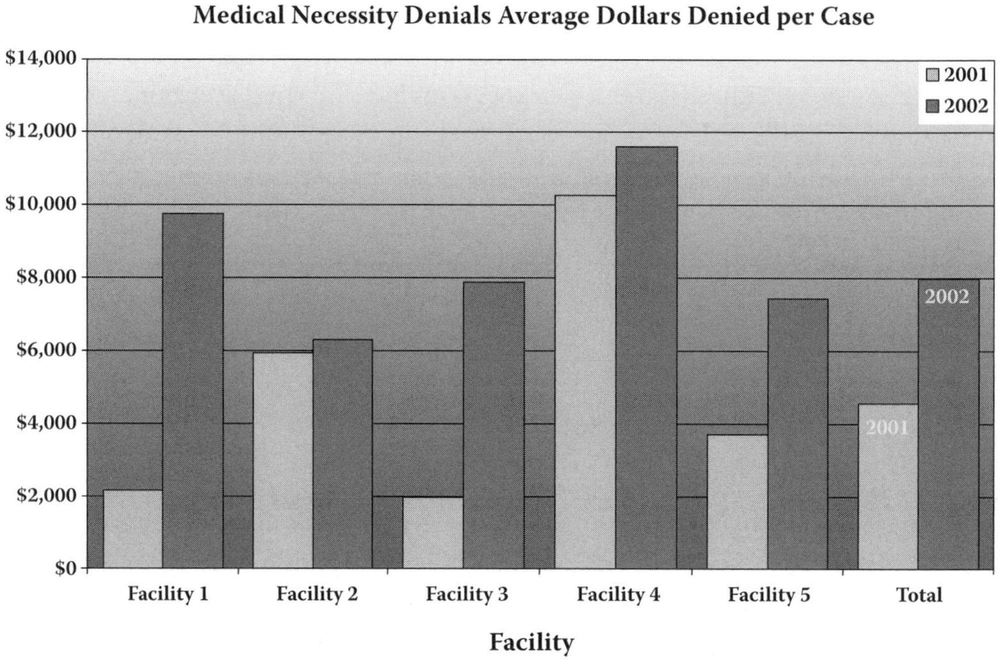

Medical Necessity Denials Average Dollars Denied per Case

Figure 4.10   Medical-necessity denials: Average dollars denied per case

these trends and the reasons for unfavorable trend lines is imperative. Minimizing dollars denied means improving bottom-line results.

Step 3: Percentage of Cases Overturned

During a 2007 case management conference, utilization-review nurses discussed the impact of the appeals process. The team estimated that it costs a hospital $500 to complete an appeals process for a denied case. Aside from the risk of not capturing the reimbursement on a case, if denied, there is an even greater risk of losing money. The ability of an appeals department to secure reimbursement is paramount. However, when the department can successfully appeal a large majority of cases, the strength of the utilization-review department should be assessed.

When the right medical information is not shared with a health plan, denials are inevitable. Not understanding the language of the health plan can result in denied claims, an increase in accounts receivables, and extra costs associated with appeals. Members of the discharge planning team must understand the criteria the health plan is using and be able to share key elements during the review process.

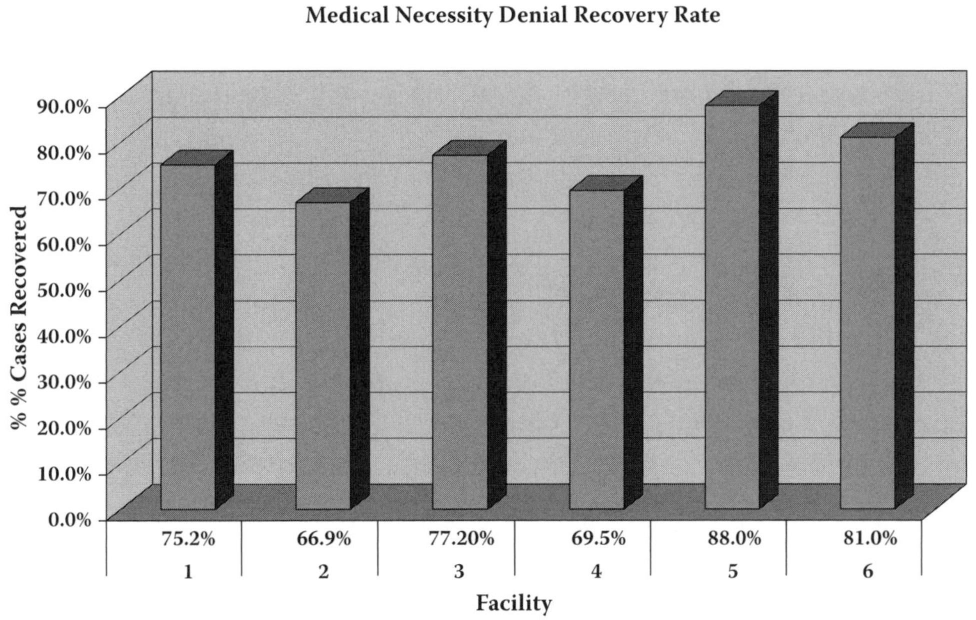

Medical Necessity Denial Recovery Rate

Figure 4.11   Medical necessity denial recovery

Figure 4.11 is a depiction of cases that were overturned during the appeals process. The overturn rate is high and may suggest a communication issue between the hospital reviewer and the health plan.

Discharge Planning Outcomes Assessment

Step 1: Readmit Rate/Reason

Monitoring and reviewing readmission data is another factor that can help determine the strength of the discharge planning process. A number of variables such as poor patient compliance, patient living alone, chronic disability, patient/physician convenience, medical quality issues, inadequate rehabilitation, and poor discharge planning can cause hospital readmissions. Readmissions are costly. It is estimated that repeated admissions may be responsible for up to 60% of hospital expenditure.[2]

Step 2: Referral Tracking

As noted, members of the discharge planning team have the ability to interface with every doctor, patient, and family member. As healthcare advocates, members of the team should be aware of post-acute-care and outpatient services. As a patient moves through the care continuum, it is vital for discharge planners to attempt to bridge any gaps in care.

Consider tracking all post-acute-care services or outpatient services that might be referred to patients while they are in the hospital. Look for services that will improve a patient's quality of care. For example, a patient with congestive heart failure, coronary artery disease, or a recent heart attack is a perfect candidate for cardiac rehabilitation. Many insurance companies cover this service. If your facility offers this service, members of your discharge planning team should be discussing this with the physician and the patient. This improves customer service by matching the patient's needs with an identified service. This also improves the patient's quality of care, reduces anxiety, and provides the patient with additional educational resources.

It is important to track the facilities that patients are selecting for post-acute-care services. Further, team members must track the reason a specific company was selected. This information may assist with providing the right intelligence to drive organizational change. For example, if data suggests that patients are selecting a competing provider because it is part of his or her provider panel, it makes sense for the hospital to evaluate the feasibility of becoming part of the provider network. This insight helps create necessary action steps to remain competitive.

Quality Assessment

Core Measures

As discussed previously, there are 26 Core Measures spread over four areas: Heart Failure, Acute Myocardial Infarction (AMI, Heart Attack), Pneumonia, and Surgical Care Implementation Project. Hospital reimbursement and quality of patient care require hospitals to manage publicly reported data for submission, to analyze the data collected, and to gain physician compliance and cooperation with these measures. Hospitals must create mechanisms to identify gaps in care and to take action prior to the patient's discharge.

Core Measure compliance has been referred to as "the open-book test that healthcare professionals keep failing." Core Measure data is beyond just the numbers. It is about meeting the minimum quality standards for the patients. The biggest challenge is that it requires accountability from multiple

Table 4.1   AMI Example: Phases of the AMI Patient

	Emergency Room	*Cardiac Cath Lab*	*Nursing Unit*	*Day of Discharge*	*Data Collection*
Clinical Action	AMI-1 Aspirin on arrival or within 24 hours	AMI-8 and AMI-8a Median time from arrival to PTCA or PCI in under 90 minutes	AMI-3 ACEI or ARB ordered	AMI-2 Aspirin at discharge	Rely on data abstraction process to identify data
Clinical Action	AMI-6 Beta Blocker on arrival		AMI-4 Smoking Cessation/ Counseling	AMI-5 Beta Blocker at Discharge	AMI-9 for JCAHO identify if patient expired
Clinical Action	AMI-7 and AMI-7a Thrombolitics under 30 minutes				

clinical professionals across multiple departments. As the patient migrates through an episode of care, all team members must be queued into action (see Table 4.1).

Table 4.1 is an example that depicts the phases a patient will experience during an AMI episode. Healthcare professionals must either address the indicator or obtain documentation from the physician that denotes why an indicator could not be met. For example, the quality standard is to give every AMI patient an aspirin within the first 24 hours of admission. However, if the patient has an allergy to aspirin, it may be contraindicated. The decision to not give aspirin is appropriate, but failure to document the clinical reason for not following the guideline results in noncompliance. Further, if data is extracted and reported incorrectly, it misrepresents the clinical care in that hospital.

In essence, hospitals must not only manage the clinical process, they must also manage collection and reporting of the data. Core Measure compliance is a hospital's "story" about its commitment to quality. Hospitals must create mechanisms to identify gaps and take necessary actions to address these issues.

Customer Service Assessment

Customer Service Survey

According to the National Research Corporation (NRC),[3] there are eight dimensions of patient-centered care:

- transition and continuity
- access to care
- coordination and integration of care
- emotional support
- information/education
- family and friend involvement
- physical comfort
- respect for patients' values, preferences, and express needs

Hospitals must take actions to ensure that they utilize a customer service satisfaction survey and respond to any aberrant service issues. As more costs and responsibility for healthcare begin to shift to the consumer, patients will be driven to shop for healthcare services based on cost, quality, and service. This fuels the demand for transparency and makes customer service and the "customer value proposition" paramount.

Hospitals need to ensure that survey questions and corresponding answer selections will provide meaningful data. Without the correct data, there is little to no business intelligence gained on which issue needs action. Physician satisfaction is another important element to track. It is important to create very concise and targeted surveys about the discharge planning department for the physicians. Customer service needs to be centered on the patients and their family members and/or significant others, as well as the physicians involved in the care of the patients.

Discharge Planning Team: COS-Q Snapshot

The COS-Q snapshot is a management tool that discharge planning depart-ments can use to quickly assess the performance of the department. These indicators have been selected based on the authors' experiences in the discharge planning function. It is based on the COS-Q quadrants of Costs, Operations, Service, and Quality. This information must be collected and tabulated at minimum on a monthly basis to provide meaningful trends.

Table 4.2 Discharge Planning COS-Q Snapshot

COSTS	OPERATIONS
Key financial metrics that impact the bottom line: • Medical-necessity data • Concurrent denial rate • Observation data • Days saved • Variance data • Appeal data • Cancelled discharge	Operational indicators that show system efficiency: • Admit trends data • EC diversion rate • EC hold times • PACU hold times • Admission delays • Discharge trends data • Bed turnover data • Average length of stay data
SERVICE	QUALITY
These are customer service scores as defined by both patients and physicians: • ALOD • Discharge delay • Initial DCP assessment • Patient satisfaction • Physician satisfaction • Referral data	These are clinical measures that generally impact the patient care: • Readmit data • Readmit reason data • Core measure compliance • Smoking cessation • Influenza vaccination • Pneumonia vaccination

Every member of the discharge planning department must be aware of these data elements. Sharing this information with staff provides an environment of open communication that fosters improvement. Consider placing each element into a snapshot summary (see Table 4.2).

Creating the data story is a key step in identifying areas needing improvement. As hospitals position for the current challenges in healthcare, members of the discharge planning team are in a unique position to become a cornerstone that drives change and impacts bottom-line results. The COS-Q snapshot provides the discharge planners with a new tool to align the discharge planning process with the strategic direction of the company.

References

1. A. Kirby and A. Kjesbo, "Tapping into Hidden Hospital Bed Capacity," Healthcare Financial Management Association, Nov. 2003; http://www.encyclopedia.com/doc/1G1-110532628.html.

2. M. Hasan, "Readmission of Patients to Hospital: Still Ill-defined and Poorly Understood," *Int. J. Qual. Health Care* 13, no. 3 (2001): 177–179.

3. National Research Corporation, NRC Picker, "Case Study: Integrating Management and Improvement," http://nrcpicker.com/Default.aspx?DN=21,2,1,Documents.

Chapter 5

Lean Concepts for Discharge Planning

Toyota revolutionized our expectations of production; Federal Express revolutionized our expectations of service. Processes that once took days or hours to complete are now measured in minutes or seconds. The challenge is to revolutionize our expectations of healthcare: to design a continuous flow of work for our clinicians and a seamless experience of care for patients.

Donald M. Berwick, M.D.
President and CEO, Institute for Healthcare Improvement

In this chapter, readers will learn:

■ the history of Lean manufacturing
■ an overview of Lean concepts
■ the seven wastes of Lean
■ popular Lean tools

Lean manufacturing concepts have origins that go back to Eli Whitney's cotton gin and interchangeable parts. This methodology was refined during the WWI and WWII for efficiently mass producing war equipment. In the 1970s it was perfected by Toyota in what is commonly referred to as "the Toyota Production System." With the tremendous success of Lean thinking in manufacturing, these performance improvement (PI) concepts have slowly migrated into healthcare. Because of the significant amount of patient and staff movement, tasks, and communication, discharge planning shows tremendous opportunities for Lean initiatives.

Overview of Lean Concepts

Lean thinking begins with the basic concept that anything that does not add value must be eliminated. Value-added steps are defined as tasks that the customer is willing to pay for, and non-value-added steps are tasks that the customer is not willing to pay for, i.e., waste. This waste is commonly referred to as *muda* (Japanese term for *waste*) in Lean.

The vast majority of consumers are accustomed to inefficiencies in their daily routines. An example is the annual car maintenance check. At a recent NASCAR race, the pit crew performed in less than 8 seconds, what would equate to 2.4 hours of billable service at the local mechanic shop. A more practical example in healthcare is the amount of wait time that is inherent in every process from registration to discharge. The bottleneck of patients waiting for services in healthcare institutions is so pervasive that it is not uncommon to find 10%–20% of service units dedicated to non-value-added waiting areas.

It is not easy identifying what is value-added and non-value-added for the patient. One method commonly used is the "customer receipt" concept. Evaluate the steps in a process and identify the tasks. Place each task on a list similar to a receipt that a customer might receive in a restaurant. Evaluate the line items from the perspective of the consumer and ask, "Is this something that a customer would pay for?"

There are five main tenets in Lean that are the drivers in developing Lean processes:

1. *Value*: The concept of value is based on providing the customer with the right product, for the right price, at the right time. The challenge is doing all of this right the first time. The application of this concept in discharge planning involves decreasing service recovery efforts and showing a one-to-one relationship between the tasks being performed and the expectations of the patient.
2. *Value Stream*: This refers to the set of actions that bring a product from conception to realization, including everything from raw materials to finished goods. The concept is visually reflected in a tool called Value Steam Mapping, which will be discussed later. The application of this

concept in discharge planning takes into account all the variables from the point that a patient event has been identified to the point of discharge. Value Stream forces the acknowledgment of the entire process.

3. *Flow*: In Lean management, all steps in the process must flow seamlessly and be complimentary and consistent. The concept of Flow in Lean thinking will potentially have the biggest impact in discharge planning functions, because current systems may be vastly unorganized and inconsistent. For example, disease-based case managers break the unit-based flow by traveling between floors to follow the patient from unit to unit.

4. *Pull*: This concept is based on acting solely to satisfy the customer's needs, rather than pushing or forcing a product or service on a customer. This forces the organization to listen to the customer's requirements and expectations. The concept of Pull forces the discharge planning staff to look at customers in a different light. With Lean thinking as applied to discharge planning, the customer can be defined not only as the patient, but also as the physician and/or other departments. The challenge in healthcare will be to balance these drivers.

5. *Perfection*: This is a quality mantra to continuously and relentlessly improve the Value Stream and flow of business operations. It is this loop-back process that incorporates Lean thinking as a part of the culture and not just a "flavor of the month" methodology. The concept of Perfection in Lean thinking changes the nature of PI in healthcare by making this a part of every employee's job description.

The Seven Wastes

Activities that add no value to the process cost the organization in terms of both dollars and time. This waste is in reality a symptom rather than a root cause of the problem. Waste points to problems within the system itself. It is imperative that, in improving the discharge planning process, all waste be identified and addressed by getting to the root of the problems. The Toyota Production System (TPS) Lean manufacturing concepts targeted seven wastes that cover virtually all means by which organizations waste or lose money; these have become known as *The Seven Wastes*.

1. *Overproduction*: Overproduction is to manufacture an item before it is actually required. Overproduction is highly costly because it prohibits the smooth flow of materials and actually degrades quality and

productivity. The TPS is also referred to as a Just in Time (JIT) system because every item is made just as it is needed. Conversely, over-production creates excessive lead times, results in high storage costs, and makes it difficult to detect defects. The solution to overproduction is reducing output. The concept is to schedule and produce only what can be immediately utilized.

An example of overproduction in healthcare is often experienced in diagnostic testing for magnetic resonance imaging (MRI). Based on the protocols of the radiologist, some organizations provide contrast for all MRI patients. It has been well documented that this process will reduce the quality of care through potential contraindications. Additionally, this reduces customer service by increasing test time for the patient and increases costs by including expensive agents that are potentially not necessary.

2. *Waiting*: Whenever goods are not moving or being processed, the waste of waiting occurs. Typically, more than 90% of a patient's process time is associated with waiting. Much of a patient's lead time is tied up in waiting for the next procedure or task. The wait time is a function of people, supplies, facility design, and technology. The ability to link pro-cesses together so that each part is connected directly into the next can dramatically reduce waiting and delays.

Delay or waiting time is so prevalent in healthcare that it is estimated that every hospital has at least 30 waiting rooms. Common delays in the discharge planning process include the time required to place the patient into a bed, and the wait time for the physical discharge after the discharge order has been written. To facilitate this process, many orga-nizations have shifted to a "patient lounge" concept to free up the bed while the patient is waiting for family or final tasks to be completed. Although this may reduce capacity issues, it does not address the root cause, which is often a lack of communication.

3. *Transporting*: Transporting products between processes is a cost that adds no value to the product or patient. Unnecessary movement and handling can cause damage and are opportunities for poor quality. By reducing the transportation of patients and supplies, organizations can reduce costs and increase the value to the patient. Healthcare has been battling the transportation of patients from floor to floor for years. As patients move from unit to unit, an incredible amount of communi-cation must occur, beds are tied up during the moves, and resources are required for bed cleanings.

4. *Inappropriate processing (overprocessing)*: There are two applications of this waste: using the wrong tools in a process and adding more value to the product or for the patient than is necessary. Many organizations choose to use expensive high-precision equipment where simpler tools would be sufficient. This often results in poor hospital layouts or costlier procedures that are unnecessary. Healthcare is driven by reimbursements. In the past, providers were given incentives to provide the costliest care available. However, in the last two decades as reimbursements have become stricter and based upon outcomes, the incentives are aligned to produce the most cost-effective method.

   In discharge planning, the case managers, utilization-review nurses, and social workers often review and document the same information on multiple forms. With the advent of electronic medical records (EMRs), once the bedside nurse enters the patient's data, it will automatically populate the required fields for all departments accessing the patient's record within the hospital, including the discharge planning department.

5. *Unnecessary inventory*: Excess inventory tends to hide problems on the plant floor, which must be identified and resolved to improve operating performance. Excess inventory increases lead times, consumes productive floor space, delays the identification of problems, and inhibits communication. By achieving a seamless flow between work centers, many manufacturers have been able to improve customer service and slash inventories and their associated costs. Work in Progress (WIP) is the work that is in various stages of production between raw material and finished product and is a measure of unnecessary inventory.

   In healthcare, batching work such as faxing to payers, lab work, or precertification processing is not uncommon. This produces the inefficiency of keeping paperwork and specimens in inventory and taking away the added potential reaction time. Keeping processes in real time is the first step toward reducing inventory.

6. *Unnecessary/excess motion*: This waste is related to ergonomics and is seen in all instances of bending, stretching, walking, lifting, and reaching. These are also health and safety issues which, in today's litigious society, are becoming more of a problem for organizations. Reducing unnecessary motion is critical in healthcare because the vast majority of employees are in high demand and at the upper salary scale.

There are many examples of excess motion in discharge planning. One common example is the movement of the utilization-review staff from floor to floor in insurance-based environments. The added motion of travel from floor to floor can add up to be a significant amount of inefficiency. In one hospital, this non-value-added task equated to one full-time equivalent (FTE) annually.

7. *Defects*: This waste involves the failure of a product to conform to specifications. Quality defects have a direct impact on the bottom line. This can result in rework, increased supply costs, and increased quality control measures. Associated costs include quarantining inventory, reinspecting, rescheduling, and capacity loss. In many organizations, the total cost of defects is often a significant percentage of total cost. Through employee involvement and Continuous Process Improvement (CPI) initiatives, there is a significant opportunity to reduce defects in many processes. There are two critical points at which a defect can be detected. A defect can be identified before the customer experiences a defective product or service. It can also be caught after the customer has experienced the defect. This often comes back in the form of customer complaints. It is desirable to identify as many defects as possible before they are experienced by the consumer.

The current healthcare system is plagued by defects in almost every function. In November 1999, the Institute of Medicine (IOM) released "To Err Is Human: Building a Safer Health System," which declared that medical errors were killing perhaps 98,000 Americans each year. An example of a defect in discharge planning is the number of on-time discharges. It is estimated that if the discharge time were decreased by 4 hours, it would be equivalent to an increase in bed capacity of 30 beds.

In recent years, an eighth waste has been commonly added to the original seven wastes, referred to as the "underutilization of staff creativity." A recent study indicated that the number one untapped resource in any organization is the mind of the employees. It is plausible to agree that no single person would know more about the nuances of any particular task than the people who are doing it day in and day out. Soliciting and creating an environment that nurtures that flow of information is the key to having a workforce that "buys in" to the changes that come with new ideas. Healthcare has started to take advantage of this resource by developing employee-involvement programs to ask staff for their opinions and ideas.

Popular Lean Tools

Financial, market, consumer, and regulatory pressures have driven many organizations to adopt Lean thinking. Healthcare has been slowly making this transition. The first step in achieving a Lean organization is to identify and attack the seven wastes. As Toyota and other world-class organizations have come to realize, customers will pay for value-added work, but never for waste. The same is true in healthcare and particularly in discharge planning. Waste is so prevalent in healthcare that Lean organizations will be able to differentiate their services easily in the marketplace.

Lean thinking provides powerful tools along with these concepts to identify and eliminate *muda*, or non-value-added tasks. Some of the most commonly used tools in Lean are: Poka-yoke (mistake proofing), Value-Stream Mapping, 5S Methodology, Spaghetti Diagram, Visual Workplace, and Kanban.

Poka-Yoke

Poka-yoke is mistake-proofing a process to prevent errors from occurring. There are six mistake-proofing principles or methods. These are listed in order of preference or precedence in fundamentally addressing mistakes:

1. *Elimination*: Eliminating the possibility of error by redesigning the product or process so that the task or part is no longer necessary.
   Example: By automating the faxing tasks in the discharge planning process, the tasks associated with the manual processing of faxes throughout the day are eliminated.
2. *Replacement*: Substituting a more reliable process to improve consistency.
   Example: In most nonautomated discharge planning systems, manual operations are developed to capture the right business intelligence. This introduces potential human errors in data processing. Automated systems can automatically run reports and analyze information with 100% accuracy in seconds, compared with what used to take days to do manually.
3. *Prevention*: Involves engineering the product or process so that it is impossible to make a mistake at all.
   Example: In discharge planning, the utilization of wrist bands is a common example of eliminating errors associated with patient identity.

4. *Facilitation*: Employs techniques that assist in making work easier to perform.

Example: Visual controls including color-coding of patients' paths to critical departments are a key concept that has been used in healthcare for years. Resealable plastic bags in the pharmacy often use color codes to designate open and closed seals.

5. *Detection*: Involves identifying an error before further processing occurs so that the user can quickly correct the problem.

Example: Order-entry systems in healthcare have developed protocols that identify and stop contraindicated medications as ordered by the physician for any patient. This system allows the error to be identified immediately and stopped for further analysis before processing.

6. *Mitigation*: Seeks to minimize the effects of errors.

Example: Mitigation has become prevalent in hospital diagnostic areas with the advent of Picture Archiving and Communication Systems (PACS). Using system "windowing" (ability to lighten or darken images), images that were captured incorrectly can be adjusted without exposing the patient to more radiation.

Mistake-proofing is the concept of engineering processes and products to eliminate the possibility of errors by the user. Common examples of designs that utilize mistake-proofing are evident in basic everyday tasks, such as putting gas in your car. Gas caps are now designed to be tethered to the automobile to prevent the driver from driving off without the cap. Furthermore, the gas cap is ratcheted to prevent overtightening using clicks. The nozzle is sized to prevent the driver from putting in the wrong type of fuel (i.e., unleaded vs. diesel). Practical utilization of this tool in healthcare is based on Computerized Order Entry (COE) systems. This system design uses business logic and red flags to prevent physicians from ordering a drug that may be contraindicated to other drugs currently being provided to the patient.

Value Stream Mapping

The difference between VSM and the traditional workflow is that additional information about each task is attached to show efficiency through metrics such as volumes, delays, and resources for each task. There are three critical components that differentiate a value map from a traditional workflow:

1. Identify the steps in the entire process from suppliers to customers.
2. Keep it high-level.
3. Add pertinent information such as time/delays/defects below each task.

Using this tool the entire system is evaluated for flow and critical efficiency data. Bottlenecks and variation in processes are quickly identified and prioritized for opportunity assessment. The critical variable in making the VSM useful is in the utilization of pertinent information about each task. Many process engineers in the healthcare industry believe that VSM is one of the most powerful tools in Lean.

5S Methodology

One of the easiest tools in the Lean tool chest is the 5S Methodology. It is a philosophy that helps organize and manage the workspace and workflow with the intent to improve efficiency by eliminating waste. It is simple and provides quick results by improving on-time delivery, quality, staff productivity, and lead times. Additionally, it decreases waste in materials, space and time, inventory, storage costs, and change-over time. The 5S Methodology is built on organization and has five main tenets:

1. *Sort*: Organize the work area by sorting and keeping what is necessary and relocating or discarding what is not. The application of this principle is very simple—keep the work space free of clutter. Only keep charts, paperwork, a laptop, and any other tool required to do the task at hand. All other inventory must be stored away.

   For discharge planning departments that are not automated, managing the paperwork process is a nightmare. Team members each carry folders filled with "cases" that contain documentation about aspects of the patient's discharge planning needs, insurance approvals, and medical justification for the hospital stay. Developing a systematic way to sort various forms and arrange them in a manner that provides ease of accessibility is critical to minimizing time lost searching for different tools.

2. *Set in order / Set limits*: Arrange needed items so they are easy to find, use, and return to streamline production in order to eliminate time spent searching for them.

   An example in discharge planning is to be sure that all required forms and documents are located in the same location at each workstation. There should be enough forms to cover the average work week. This keeps consistency and efficiency in the workstation while promoting a clean and organized work environment.

3. *Shine and inspect through cleaning*: Clean and care for equipment and work areas, and inspect while doing so. The application of this concept is very important in healthcare, since the spread of infectious diseases and contaminants to patients is a serious problem.

   Discharge planning departments are often confined to very small and crowded office spaces. Keeping the area free from mounds of disorganized paperwork by having items filed neatly is key to promoting a cleaner and employee-friendly work environment. This also promotes easy visualization of and access to information needed to perform the job task.

4. *Standardize*: Make all work areas similar so that procedures are obvious and instinctual, and defects stand out. By standardizing all processes across all employees, variation is reduced and issues are easily replicable. Once issues can be predicted and tracked, then they can be managed. Tools such as control limits (a trending graph that shows allowable min or max points with any metric before a flag is raised) can be used to keep processes consistent.

   Standardization is one of the most important opportunities in the discharge planning department. Utilizing a standardized work tool such as an initial discharge planning screen is one example where processes are formalized and defects minimized. A standardized screen can promote early identification of discharge planning needs and minimize the risk of reactive discharge planning and patients falling through the cracks.

5. *Sustain*: Make the new processes natural and part of the culture. Sustainability is a key part of any changes, either through Lean or Six Sigma. It is imperative to sustain the gain.

   During a clinical documentation program implementation, the program was expected to identify improved reimbursement opportunities. When the program was implemented, team members participated in setting targets and meeting on a monthly basis to evaluate their progress. The department accepted accountability for the target and worked to maintain the gain. The program has been in operation for over seven years and has consistently contributed significant dollars in reimbursement.

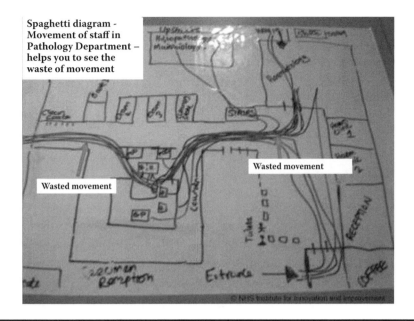

Spaghetti diagram - Movement of staff in Pathology Department – helps you to see the waste of movement

Wasted movement

Wasted movement

Figure 5.1   Example of a spaghetti diagram completed in the Pathology department to determine the movement of physicians and patients

Because the 5S process is so simple, most healthcare organizations are opting to start with this tool in moving toward a culture of Lean thinking. Often, most departments complement the 5S process by enhancing it with other Lean tools. For example, in determining the waste of movement and designing a process to set it in order, a tool called the Spaghetti Diagram is used.

Spaghetti Diagram

The spaghetti diagram starts with a layout of the workstations. During a particular shift, all movement of the staff or the product is tracked. Once the movements have been drawn out, it generally resembles a plate of spaghetti, hence the term *spaghetti diagram*. Figure 5.1 illustrates an example of a spaghetti diagram completed in the Pathology department to determine the movement of the physicians and patients. The flow of people and products from station to station helps identify any non-value-added steps or travel that is occurring in the process for elimination.

Visual Workplace

Another tool that complements the 5S method is the Visual Workplace. With this concept, visual effects are used to quickly communicate pertinent information. For example, keys can be color-coded so that staff members are not flipping though the entire key chain to find the right key. The most common visual workplace elements in healthcare are often found in the patient chart through colored tabs and forms. This assists the providers in quickly sifting through data to find the right category of information or quickly identifying pertinent issues such as Core Measures, medical necessity status, and pharmacy notification.

Kanban

Kanban is one of the cornerstones of Lean manufacturing. Kanban is a visual scheduling system that enables the process owner to easily view production requirements of individual parts and machines. There are many examples of visual cues in the discharge planning department. For example, color-coded cues help address physician Core Measure compliance. Team members place different colored sheets in the medical record to prompt physicians to document required information for governmental compliance. These are simple mechanisms that serve as prompters or reminders with the expectation that a task needs to be accomplished.

Often referred to as the "nervous system" of Lean production, Kanban is a key technique that determines a process production quantity and, in doing so, facilitates JIT production and ordering systems. Contrary to more traditional "push" methods of mass production, which are based on an estimated number of expected sales, Kanban's "pull" system creates greater flexibility on the production floor, such that the organization only produces what is ordered. Kanban directly applies to discharge planning, since it is purely a function of steps that trigger events toward the final product: discharge. There are four important rules for Kanban.

1. Kanban works from upstream to downstream in the production process. This means that the customer, at each step of the process, is driving every deliverable. At each step, only as many parts are withdrawn as the Kanban instructs, helping to ensure that only what is ordered is made. The necessary parts in a given step always accompany the Kanban to ensure visual control.
2. The upstream processes only produce what has been withdrawn. This includes only producing items in the sequence in which they are received on the Kanban, and only producing the number indicated on the Kanban.

3. Only products that are defect free continue on through the production line. In this way, each step uncovers and then corrects the defects that are found, before any more can be produced.

4. The number of Kanbans should be decreased over time. Minimizing the total number of Kanbans is the best way to uncover areas of needed improvement. By constantly reducing the total number of Kanbans, continuous improvement is facilitated by concurrently reducing the overall level of stock in production.

The House of Lean

All of the aforementioned Lean-thinking tools are put together into a consolidated format commonly referred to as the "House of Lean." The foundation is based on the Value Stream analysis and the information that it captures about the entire system. There are three pillars: flow and pull; employee involvement; and value and perfection. The outcome of these tools and processes is represented by the "roof" of the house through the identification of "best in quality," "lowest in cost," and "shortest lead time."

Lean fits very well into the Six Sigma methodology, which will be discussed in Chapter 10. Six Sigma is the delivery methodology because of its disciplined approach. Lean thinking enhances Six Sigma by becoming the solutions engine that produces practical ideas for improvement in operations. Hence, most organizations refer to these initiatives as Lean Six Sigma programs.

Because Lean thinking can be intimidating to most organizations, the utilization of consultants for the initial engagement is highly recommended. Lean concepts are basic and visual in nature, and can be picked up very quickly by most prudent managers and directors. It is important to make every effort to make the first initiative a success so that it can set the stage for replication across the organization. Alternatively, if the product is used incorrectly and consequently fails to achieve its objectives, then it may present an uphill battle from that point to implement Lean initiatives.

Based on the current drivers of healthcare, the utilization of Lean-thinking concepts will only increase in the healthcare industry. The advantages of this tool are that it is practical in nature, it keeps employees involved, it produces results quickly, and it is highly visual.

Chapter 6

The Top 10 Secrets to a
New Revenue Pipeline

There is no shame in not knowing; the shame lies in not finding out.

Russian proverb

In this chapter, readers will learn:

- the top 10 secrets to a new revenue pipeline
- the application of Lean principles to unlock revenue
- how other hospitals have been successful in applying Lean principles

Lean thinking is a new concept in healthcare and can initially be intimidating for most staff and managers. To provide a jump start, the authors have identified the top 10 applications of Lean principles in specific discharge planning processes. These secrets to a new revenue pipeline are the result of 25 years of performance improvement (PI) experience in discharge planning.

Secret 1: Less Is More

- *Lean principle*: Lean principles consider discharge planning models that eliminate redundant and non-value-added tasks for optimization. Therefore, reducing redundancies (extra steps), streamlining communication (handoffs), and minimizing staff movement (motion) create the optimal platform for redesign.

■ *Application*: Chapter 1 provided examples of model configuration and discussed the results of a literature review of different discharge planning models. The two models reviewed were the dyad and triad models. In a dyad model, there are two members involved in the department: a utilization-review nurse and a social worker. In the triad model, there are three members involved: a case manager, a utilization-review nurse, and a social worker.

■ *Evidence*: Hospitals that have triad models may experience overlapping and redundancy in functions. During a 2006 assessment in a 300+-bed hospital, a survey was conducted with the case managers, social workers, and utilization-review nurses of the discharge planning department. The survey reviewed tasks completed on a daily basis. The results demonstrated significant overlap in their functions. For example, every member of the team conducted a review of the medical record, participated in multidisciplinary rounds, and interacted with both physicians and members of the healthcare team.

After review, a subcommittee was formed, and the team recommended a consolidated model. The new model (a dyad model) consisted of an RN care coordinator and a social worker. The team also assigned set ratios of one RN to 25 beds and one social worker to 50 beds. The new model eliminated the need for a social worker and a nurse. This organization opted to shift those staff members to the emergency center to provide care-coordination services for that department. Team members were more satisfied with the streamlined process, reductions in redundancy, and improved coordination. Other members of the healthcare team reported improved communication (only two people to interact with vs. three) and improved access to the workstation and medical records (due to fewer people accessing computers and medical records in the unit). This model reduces the redundancy of chart review, the collection of duplicative information, the required amount of communication or handoffs, and the number of extra steps in the process.

■ *Benefits realization*: The labor expense for the social worker was estimated to be $21.50/hour and for the nurse it was estimated to be $26.50/hour. Benefits were factored in at 27%. Annualized, the labor expense was reduced by $126,797. In this scenario, the hospital elected to shift resources to the emergency center.

Secret 2: Put "Aces" in Their Places

■ *Lean principle*: Lean thinking targets unnecessary staff or product movements for elimination at every opportunity. As explained in Chapter 1, based on the configuration of the team (disease-based, unit-based, or physician-based), travel time between patients can vary among discharge planning employees.

■ *Application*:

– Disease based: While there is great credence in the value of having clinical experts aligned with a particular diagnosis, this model would not be considered Lean. Take, for example, a renal nurse coordinator in one facility who interacted with every dialysis, pre-renal failure patient in a 700+-bed hospital. The hospital had nine floors and two main elevator sets. Traveling from unit to unit was difficult, and interacting with physicians and the ancillary work team was also quite difficult. The nurse could not attend every interdisciplinary rounds session, and therefore critical information about the discharge plans were not well communicated. This configuration created extra steps to process discharges, created excessive motion, resulted in patients having to wait for information, and produced significant handoff concerns.

– Physician based: The physician-based team configuration mirrors the same issues as the disease-based model. It is difficult to manage, creates redundancy, and impacts productivity. Typically, staff members are employed by the hospital, yet their job function is to support the physician and assist with bridging information between the physician's office and the hospital. While this helps expedite discharges, the benefits are greater for the physician and patient, and do not always tie in with the driving organizational change. According to Lean principals, this configuration would be considered suboptimal.

– Unit based: A unit-based team configuration would assign one nurse to each unit or group of beds. From a clinical perspective, utilizing a nurse who has a clinical background similar to the unit would be the most advantageous. This design would reduce waste, add value, and be considered optimal.

■ *Evidence*: A recent time study, conducted at the same 700+-bed tertiary-care center mentioned previously, revealed significant opportunities to reduce travel time by changing to a unit-based team configuration. The facility's multiple floors and varying bed capacity per unit/floor were significant factors impacting the decision to change. This facility utilized a triad model, with case managers, utilization review, and social-work services. Team members were configured in a manner to provide unit-based, physician-based, and disease-based support. A portion of the social-work members and case managers were assigned as disease-based team members. The study demonstrated that six full-time positions were lost due to the wait times at elevators, traveling up and down stairs, and attempting to gather information that was missed during unit rounds. Adopting a unit-based design with nurses who had a strong clinical background in the assigned units created the best value for the organization.

■ *Benefits realization*: The mean income per employee was estimated to be approximately $54,000/year. Once benefits were factored in (at 27%), the annual average labor expense was estimated to be $68,530 per employee. If the tertiary-care center eliminated the wasted labor expense, this could represent an annual savings of $411,180. In this scenario, resources were shifted to other areas of the hospital that demonstrated need.

Secret 3: Learn the Language of the Payer

■ *Lean principle*: Lean principles would consider any process that resulted in rework to be suboptimal. Discharge planning departments that do not have utilization-review team members trained in the standardized criteria used by various health plans in their market are not positioned to "speak the language" of the payer. This can result in costly denials and increased rework on the back end during the appeals process.

■ *Application:* Adopting a standard set of clinical guidelines for acute-care bed utilization is one of the most important tasks in strengthening the discharge planning department. These guidelines assist those performing the utilization-review function by providing sets of measurable, clinical, diagnostic, or therapeutic indicators that reflect a patient's need for hospitalization. Team members are able to consistently apply evidenced-based and best-practice guidelines for care-related decisions, while considering the individual needs of the patient in partnership with the knowledge and skills of the physician and ancillary team members.

A complete understanding and consistent interpretation of the payer's criteria are essential. Internal audits must be performed within the team to ensure departmental compliance. Additionally, it is important for physicians to understand basic concepts regarding the criteria used to determine severity of illness and intensity of service.

■ *Evidence:* During a 2005 assessment of an integrated delivery system (IDS) with five participating hospitals, it was discovered that the IDS received over 700 medical-necessity denials for the year. On average, the IDS was able to reverse approximately 55% of the denials received. Members of the denial team were asked for input on how to decrease the denial rate. The lead denial coordinator discovered that most denials were the result of poor communication of clinical issues from the utilization-review team member to members of the health plan. These failures in communication resulted in multiple denials.

Further, it was determined that team members were using outdated criteria and had no formal process to audit and control the application of the guidelines. This resulted in the adoption of standardized criteria and a policy for application of the guideline, as well as audits for compliance. One hospital achieved a 20% reduction in denials year over year for 2005 and 2006. Plans are to use the same approach throughout the health system.

■ *Benefits realization:* The IDS estimated that each medical-necessity denial cost approximately $500 per appeal in labor and administrative supplies. If a hospital performed 700 appeals in one year, the cost would amount to $350,000. Thus, improving front-end communication reduces rework and supply costs.

Secret 4: Understand Medicare Observation Status

■ *Lean principle:* The Lean concept of *standardization* within the 5S methodology (see Chapter 5) is a major driver in creating a consistent approach to the application of a standard-criterion tool to manage observation patients.

■ *Application:* Understanding the use of observation status is critical for a number of reasons, but for our purposes we will narrow our focus to two specific reasons: wrong classifications and failure to bill ancillary charges. Both will impact reimbursement.

– Classification: Observation status is an administrative classification of patients who are registered in an emergency room or outpatient clinic, and whose condition is uncertain but warrants closer observation. Patients requiring 6–24 hours of care may be placed in a hospital bed without a formal admission. Some important points to remember regarding observation status as are follows:

- Intended for short term monitoring, generally less than 24 hours.
- Services are reimbursed under the Outpatient Prospective Payment System (OPPS).
- If utilized for patients with chest pain, congestive heart failure, or asthma, services are paid under specific Ambulatory Payment Classifications (APCs). Patients must receive treatment for 8–48 hours.
- There must be a specific order from the physician for designation of observation status. Failure to designate status can result in the "take back" of dollars paid.
- The clock starts when the patient is placed in the unit and ends when the nurse signs off on the discharge.
- The hospital is only reimbursed for up to 48 hours, which should be an exception rather than the rule.
- Ancillary billing for a specific service is acceptable if documented in the medical record.
- The patient can be progressed to inpatient status if his or her condition meets the inpatient level of care.
- The patient's status can be converted by the hospital using Condition Code 44 if the hospital utilization-review committee makes the determination prior to discharge. (The physician must concur with the decision of the committee, and documentation must be obtained.)

Discharge planning team members must be certain that they are applying standard medical-necessity guidelines to ensure that the correct status has been utilized (inpatient vs. observation). According to some hospitals, getting the decision right is essential to ensure revenue integrity. It has been suggested at the Observation Symposium 2008 that, on average, Medicare pays about $5,000 more for an inpatient than for an outpatient, so billing one legitimate inpatient stay as observation status every day could add up to more than $1 million in lost revenue each year.

- Ancillary charges: The second part of this secret deals with the proper billing of ancillary charges for patients in observation status. When patients are in observation status, specific documentation must be in the medical record in order to be reimbursed for charges. Failure to secure the necessary documentation results in lost revenue.

■ *Evidence*: In 2003, one hospital utilization manager noted that 18%–22% of discharges were observation cases. The hospital typically carried 500 Medicare discharges per month. After review of standard criteria, it was determined that many of the patients met medical necessity for an inpatient level of care. The manager worked with the utilization-review team members to improve processes to reclassify patients who should be moved from observation status to inpatient status. By the end of the year, observation discharges had been effectively reduced to 12%.

In 2006, this same hospital struggled with the processes needed to capture lost revenue for ancillary charges. The finance department contacted the utilization-review manager for suggestions on how to capture these charges. The utilization-review manager suggested centralizing the function under one team member from the department who had been trained in the process of managing observation conversions. This person would now be responsible for both observation conversions and capturing ancillary charges for patients in observation status. The process was very successful and yielded over $1.2 million in captured revenues during the first nine months of the program.

- *Benefits realization*: Conservatively, noting the reduction in observation cases from 18% to 12% is substantial. There were roughly 6,000 Medicare patients discharged from this facility in 2003. Through the application of *standardized* clinical guidelines, patients' statuses were reassigned based on medical necessity. This data suggests that observation cases went from 1080 to 720 cases. Therefore, 360 cases were shifted to inpatient status. As noted, on average, Medicare pays $5,000 more per inpatient, which in this case amounted to recapturing $1.8 million. Improved capture of ancillary charges also recovered an additional $1.2 million in less than nine months when processes were put in place to centralize this function and standardize the processes. Thus the hospital gained a total of $3 million in recaptured revenue after standardizing processes for patients in observation status.

Secret 5: Attack Variance Days

- *Lean principle*: Patients that stay longer than medically necessary in an acute-care setting are considered victims of overprocessing or delays according to Lean methodology. This includes delay of the patient going to the next level of care, and overprocessing of the patient with services that are not required.
- *Application*: Avoidable days are unnecessary days that make a patient's hospital stay longer. Some of the disadvantages of a longer length of stay (LOS) include increased risk of infection and waste of healthcare

resources. Discharge planning team members are often aware of these avoidable days and can easily identify common areas for improvement. As discussed in Chapter 3 and Chapter 4, variance days impact costs, operations, service, and quality of care (COS-Q).

■ *Evidence*: In 2002, a 700+-bed tertiary-care center began a program to identify avoidable days. The impetus behind the program was due to the identification of increased emergency room diversions, capacity constraints, and customer dissatisfaction. Members of the discharge planning team defined and categorized avoidable days, and then collected and collated the data. During the first year of the program, the hospital identified over 3,000 avoidable days that could be impacted by members of the discharge planning team. There were five target areas identified: physician barriers to discharge, failed timely discharge planning, delays due to family members, availability of a skilled nursing facility, and internal step-down bed availability. Once target areas were identified, members of the discharge planning team designed processes to minimize and impact these variances. Avoidable days that were minimized were tracked and recorded as "days saved." In 2002, there were approximately 500 "days saved," and by 2006 the impact had increased to 1,100 "days saved."

■ *Benefits realization*: Based upon a 2006 throughput analysis conducted by John C. Lincoln Health System, average direct costs per day can be reduced by $420/day if "impacted." The aforementioned hospital reduced avoidable occurrences by 1,100 days in 2006, resulting in a cost reduction of $462,000.

Secret 6: Capture the Flag

■ *Lean principle*: The principle of defects can apply to many aspects of discharge planning. The most valuable application is in the documentation of completed work. There is a direct correlation between minimal documentation and minimal reimbursement.

■ *Application*: Members of the discharge planning team or coding team often "flag" or identify poor clinical documentation in the medical record. Failure to obtain appropriate documentation can result in the loss of millions of dollars. Members of the discharge planning team must not only create the flag, but must also be sure to capture the reimbursement.

    This is best accomplished by implementing a Clinical Documentation Management Program (CDMP). CDMP improves quality of care (through physician documentation of diagnosis and co-morbid conditions), assists with matching the appropriate rate of reimbursement to actual services rendered to a patient during hospitalization, and promotes CMS (Centers for Medicare and Medicaid Services) compliance. Diagnosis-Related Groups (DRGs) is a system implemented by CMS in the early 1980s and was designed to classify hospital cases into groups expected to have similar hospital resource consumption. This system was developed for Medicare as part of the perspective payment system.

For fiscal year 2008, the acute-care hospital Inpatient Prospective Payment System (IPPS) was further developed. The final rule was published in the Federal Register on August 22, 2007. The rule implemented Medicare Severity-adjusted Diagnosis-Related Groups (MS-DRGs), which now replace the current 538 CMS DRGs with 745 MS-DRGs.

The MS-DRGs are based on the current CMS DRGs. The MS-DRGs can be divided into a maximum of three payment tiers based on the severity or presence of a major complication: co-morbidity, complication code, or no complication code. CDMP requires a concerted effort by physicians, utilization-review experts, and coding professionals to adhere to detailed documentation records.

■ *Evidence*: In 2000, a 700+-bed tertiary-care center implemented a CDMP program. Key to the program was the hiring of a DRG-educator employee. The DRG educator worked on developing policy, creating data tracking and compliance audits, and worked with both the coding professionals and utilization-review team members to set targets and communicate outcomes. On an annual basis, the team identified an average of 700–800 opportunities to align medical documentation with resources consumed. In many cases, this resulted in an increase in DRG payments.

■ *Benefits realization*: Hospitals that do not have CDMP programs are estimated to have a 10%–20% opportunity to improve clinical documentation. In the aforementioned tertiary-care center, the opportunity averaged 11%–15% from years 2000 to 2007. Annual reimbursement dollars captured by the members of the utilization-review team ranged from $750,000 to $1.2 million.

Secret 7: Learn to Tell Your Story

■ *Lean principle*: Adding value to the customer experience is a cornerstone of Lean thinking. This can be applied toward processes in discharge planning that provide services that were previously unknown to the patient. Lean thinking shows that every opportunity should be taken to add value for the patient.

■ *Application*: Members of the discharge planning department interact with almost every patient who enters the hospital. Team members are often focused on providing patients with programs that improve their quality of life as they transition to home or to the next level of care. They often feel that they are the advocate for the patient, yet often they are not informed of programs or services available. This team, if focused correctly, can act as a bridge connecting patient needs with services that a hospital or integrated delivery system can provide. It is critical to ensure that members of the discharge planning department be aware of services they can offer to the patient. It is also important that they have a mechanism to track the referrals that they make to the patient.

CMS guidelines require the discharge planner to present options to the patient and family. The patient must always be given a "choice" to select the post-acute-care provider. Discharge planners are able to discuss internal services with the patient as long as the patient is informed of the affiliation. Many hospitals provide a number of services that patients simply are not aware of, such as:

  – diabetes education classes
  – smoking-cessation programs
  – weight-loss-management programs
  – cardiac rehab
  – pulmonary rehab
  – home-care services
  – home-IV services
  – durable medical equipment
  – pharmacy services
  – transportation services

Aside from providing increases in downstream revenue, this is a great opportunity to create a strong feedback loop with your patients. If there are problems, they should be directed to the discharge planning department. This allows for information to be communicated to the post-acute-care service provider. When an internal program is utilized, the company can gain insight into problem areas and further address and strengthen its program. This is also a great service-recovery tool and provides companies with an opportunity to gain and maintain market and customer share.

Outpatient diagnostic procedures such as magnetic resonance imaging (MRI), computed tomography (CT), and nuclear medicine procedures yield some of the highest margins. It is imperative for hospitals to begin assisting with the coordination of these services. This can improve customer service, quality of care, and profit margins. Depending on the aggressiveness of the market, hospitals must be diligent in securing the downstream revenue. This is even more imperative in IDSs.

- *Evidence*: In a 365+-bed hospital located in a rural area, a committee evaluated the number of Medicare admissions it was losing when patients were discharged to skilled-nursing facilities for long-term placement. The team determined that once the patient transferred, if the patient needed additional services, business was shifted to competing hospitals. On average, 70% of patients were lost to the market competitor. The duration of the study was approximately five years. Members of the senior-service division noted that this caused great dissatisfaction for the patients and for the physicians. In 1999, the hospital created a gerontology group that would bridge the care continuum from hospital to long-term-care provider. When patients needed additional medical services, the gerontologist coordinated an admission to the hospital where the patient's physician practiced. This process returned the admission back to the hospital and improved the quality of care for the patient.

  Initially, discharge planners did not understand the value of the program. In the first three months, referrals averaged fewer than three per month. After the discharge planners, medical executive committee, and the larger physician practice groups were educated on the project, the referrals increased to over 20 patients in the program in the next month. Referrals in the subsequent months increased to 60 and totaled 120 patients in the subsequent year.

- *Benefits realization*: In 1999, CMS estimated that the average annual payment for medical services per patient totaled approximately $1,300. This suggests that the hospital could potentially generate an additional $156,000 in revenue.

Secret 8: The 48-Hour Drill

- *Lean principle:* There are many work tools that can be developed and used to assist members of the discharge planning team with completing the daily tasks required. Lean-thinking principles dictate that tools need to be developed to minimize redundancies, decrease unnecessary steps, and create value for the patient.

■ *Application*: Creation of work tools and checklists have proved to yield significant improvements in work flow. The first step in hardwiring excellence in care is ensuring a systematic review of needs, with a mechanism to ensure that all of the patient's needs are addressed. In discharge planning departments, there are multiple priorities that must be addressed as the patient moves through the care continuum. In the absence of technology, manual processes may be fragmented or vary from unit to unit. The development of checklists minimizes time, reduces variation, and improves coordination of care. Some examples of checklists are:

- Admission-review checklist for the RN-care coordinator:
  - application of criteria and necessary actions
  - observation review (if required)
  - application of CDMP (if required)
  - Core Measure review (if applicable)
  - smoking-cessation review (if applicable)
  - pneumonia/influenza vaccination review
  - initial discharge planning assessment and identification of high-risk indicators (interview with patient)
  - social-work referral for complex discharge planning (triggered by identification of a high-risk indicator)
- Interdisciplinary-care-rounds checklist:
  - Core Measure review and education (if applicable)
  - discharge plans
  - targeted length of stay
  - barriers to discharge planning
  - medications needed at discharge
  - transportation needed at discharge
  - clinical reasons as they relate to discharge
  - orders needed for discharge
- Day-before-discharge checklist:
  - prescriptions required
  - important information from Medicare served (as applicable)
  - transportation arrangement confirmed
  - community-referral forms and transfer-certification forms completed as required

- Day-of-discharge checklist:
  - medication reconciliation
  - final check of all documents
  - discharge instructions and education from bedside RN
  - follow-up appointment or final discharge plans communicated

■ *Evidence*: In 2006, a 365+-bed hospital implemented these aforementioned work tools. The team used the 48-hour marker as a trigger. When team members reasonably assumed a discharge was going to occur in 48 hours or less, they became more focused on ensuring that the patient was prepared for discharge. The goal of the pilot study was focused on improving 11 indicators, two of which were focused on increasing staff productivity and processing discharges in a more timely manner. A baseline assessment was completed, and the results revealed that the average length of discharge (ALOD) was approximately 4 hours and 43 minutes. The average social-work caseload was 14 patients a day. After six weeks of implementation, the ALOD decreased by 33 minutes, and the social-worker caseload increased to 18 patients per day. Team members reported that multidisciplinary rounds were more streamlined, handoffs were more controlled, and there were obvious delays noted when patients were transferred in from other units where the pilot study was not being conducted. This pilot study also demonstrated a favorable trend line for 9 of 11 targeted outcomes.

■ *Benefits realization*: The hospital estimated that, on the day of discharge, a minute represented $6.25 in costs. If the average discharge decreased by 33 minutes, this resulted in a cost savings of $206.25 per discharge. Data was extrapolated against projected annual discharges, which was estimated at 11,000. The hospital made the assumption that approximately 25% of discharges could be impacted. The projected cost savings were $567,187.

Secret 9: Know the Code

■ *Lean principle*: The Lean principle of waste (*muda*) elimination requires that every effort be made to complete the task correctly the first time. This concept is applicable in many aspects of discharge planning, but most importantly in making sure the discharge status codes are correct.

■ *Application*: Hospitals are responsible for ensuring that the patient status codes are reported accurately on the billing claim. Inaccurate admission or discharge-destination codes may result in payment errors and the "take back" of reimbursement. A patient-status code is a two-digit code that identifies where the patient is at the conclusion of a healthcare facility encounter (could be a visit or an actual inpatient stay) or at the end of a billing cycle (the "through" date of a claim). The code is placed on the UB-92 and used for billing purposes. Omitting the code or submitting a claim with the incorrect code is a claim billing error and could result in the claim being rejected, resulting in payment "take back."

■ *Evidence*: In 2002, members of a discharge planning team noted the "take back" of dollars from CMS for inaccurate discharge planning codes being assigned at the time of discharge. The team reviewed the cases denied and determined that there was confusion in the assignments. Medical-records specialists reviewed the cases and assigned the code; however, the social-work documentation made it difficult to determine the actual discharge status. Members of the team developed a discharge-summary report. The report was set up in a check-box format, and the discharge planner was assigned the responsibility of checking off the discharge status (which included the two-digit code) at the time of discharge. Unit clerks, discharge planners, and coding professionals were all given cue cards that specified the two-digit code and the corresponding definition. Once initiated, coding professionals were able to easily identify the discharge status.

During the initial quarter, there were seven cases denied for payment. After implementation, the cases decreased to three, and in the last quarter there were no denials. While the number of cases denied may seem insignificant, the total dollar amount denied for the first and second quarters was $292,024.

■ *Benefits realization*: For benefits realization, it is important to note that these dollars have already been collected. The purpose is to not lose this revenue through an audit. Additionally, at times CMS allows for ancillary charges to be billed after the initial "take back." Nonetheless, a heightened awareness must be placed on knowing, understanding, and assigning the correct patient status at the time of admission and discharge.

Secret 10: Be Aggressive (Proactive Denial Management)

■ *Lean principle*: Rework in Lean is a major category of waste. It crosses every aspect of the COS-Q from quality of the product to service. Most importantly, it adds costs that the customer is not willing to pay for. The best application of this concept in discharge planning is in the service-denials function. By streamlining the processes up front, the wasted rework on the back end is eliminated.

■ *Application*: Managed care denials due to lack of medical necessity profoundly affect the bottom line of hospitals throughout the United States. Payment management and denial elimination are key components of an effective revenue-cycle process. Denials effectively delay or eliminate payment and represent high financial risk to the organization.

Payers constantly find reasons to deny or underpay claims and delay payment. Tracking and analyzing payment and denial patterns can make the difference between financial stability and failure. Effective denial management demands a committed team approach.

Aside from managing average length of stay (ALOS) through the application of standardized criteria, members of the discharge planning team must also aggressively manage concurrent denials. Concurrent denials are denials that occur while the patient is still in the hospital. They can be in the form of underpayment of claims (payer requesting that an inpatient be converted to observation) or denial for payment. Implementing standard criteria, developing concurrent denial-reversal processes, and evaluating every conversion request against the medical-necessity criteria can effectively reduce denials.

Standard criteria guide utilization-review team members. When criteria begin to diminish and the patient becomes medically stable, a discharge should be facilitated. Concurrent denial-reversal processes are aggressive actions taken by the utilization-review team member. Once a concurrent denial is given, the team members request a physician-to-physician interaction. The hope is that the attending or consulting physician (or in some cases the physician adviser) is able to provide additional medical information of justification to the physician (medical director) of the health plan.

At times, payers may request that a case be converted to observation status. When this occurs, utilization-review team members must ensure that the conversion meets medical-necessity guidelines. Failure to review can result in the loss of revenue.

■ *Evidence*: In 2004, a tertiary-care center in Cincinnati implemented an aggressive denial-management program. Phase 1 included adopting standardized, clinically based medical criteria that served as guidelines for acute-care utilization. Phase 2 included utilizing the physician adviser to serve as a liaison between the hospital and the health plan. When a concurrent denial took place, the physician adviser was notified. The physician then reviewed the medical record and communicated with the health plan. Phase 3 involved education and process development to manage inpatient-to-observation-conversion requests. These cases were evaluated against a criterion for medical necessity prior to converting. If the case met the medical-necessity criterion, the utilization-review nurse did not convert the case. When the utilization-review nurse and health plan did not concur, a denial was accepted, and the appeal department was notified in an effort to prepare for the appeal process.

■ *Benefits realization*: The hospital achieved:
  – a 47% decrease in dollars denied (net change of $171,251 fewer dollars denied)
  – a 41% decrease in cases denied (net change of 41 cases denied)
  – a decrease in the inpatient-to-observation conversion rate for one health plan from 95% to 55% (616 fewer patients converted from inpatient to observation status)

Conclusion

The secret to unlocking the discharge planning revenue pipeline in any organization is knowing where to look. These top-10 secrets allow the department to accelerate the transformation process by providing insight into best practices based on 26 years of experience. Lean concepts provide the framework to evaluate inefficiencies in current practices and assist the staff in identifying opportunities. By applying Lean to these secrets, the non-value-added steps are easily identified, and action steps can be developed for improvement.

Chapter 7

The Results-Oriented Job Description

Many people fail in life, not for lack of ability or brains or even courage but simply because they have never organized their energies around a goal.

Elbert Hubbard

In this chapter, readers will learn:

- why job descriptions matter
- key definitions of job description, job focus, and job function
- key elements of a *results-oriented* job description

Why Job Descriptions Matter

In one recent study, a process engineer was challenged with assessing the discharge planning functions in a multihospital system. In the initial assessment phase, it was determined that not one of the hospitals had a single job description for utilization-review nurses, case managers, social workers, or discharge planners that matched. If this problem exists within an IDS (integrated delivery system, i.e., hospitals belonging to the same company), it is plausible to estimate that this variation is even more pronounced across nonaffiliated hospitals.

This variation introduces inefficiencies across many elements. Processes for the patient and staff are by default inefficient because each job description will force a different path of care. Variation of priorities for each staff member is introduced. In some organizations, Core Measures may be a priority, while in others it may be costs. This introduces an imbalance in the COS-Q (cost, operations, service, and quality of care) function. Additionally, this variation may introduce human resource issues based on standards of pay and tasks.

In hospitals that wish to gain high levels of team and systems accountability, building the right team is rooted in creating a more focused job description. Effective work teams require that expectations be shared openly with the employees. Job descriptions help employees and leaders create the foundation for a mutual understanding. These understandings are important because they can help prevent misconceptions regarding job performance in the future.

A new change in the type of job description is on the horizon—the *results-oriented* job description. When job description details are organized around performance outcomes, the following benefits can be achieved:

■ Leaders are more likely to hire the right person when both the employee and the leader clearly understand the job.
■ Team members are able to understand how they can contribute to the mission, vision, and values of the company.
■ Leaders are better able to match performance to the job description.
■ Leaders are able to defend placing an employee in positive discipline due to poor performance as noted in the job description.

Many discharge planning team members are placed in ambiguous situations where clear delineation of job function and job focus are not outlined. When team members lack job focus their "scope" of service begins to "creep" into other areas that are not essential to their job function. Lack of direction and clarity creates a pocket of ambiguity that diminishes value in the workplace. This can be avoided by implementing tools to create a solid job description with clear expectations and accountability. Simple changes in the document language can outline the job, description, focus, and function, and thus recreate the framework for effective team development and departmental success.

Job Description vs. Job Function vs. Job Focus

Most employers recognize that the key purpose of a job description is to identify the contributions required by the organization. It is also a tool to ensure that subordinates understand what they are expected to achieve, and the criteria on which their performance is assessed. But what is the relationship between *job description, job focus*, and *job function*? While there should be an interconnected relationship, more often than not there is little correlation between these elements. As the healthcare sector positions for the future, there must be a new approach to defining and creating the expectations for its employees.

A *job* can be defined as a collection of tasks and duties that an employee is responsible to perform. A *job description* is a document that describes the purpose, expected activities, and responsibilities of a particular job, and often serves as the basis for determining compensation, reviewing performance, and recruiting new hires. However, not every job description is worded in a fashion that would allow employers to effectively measure performance. A *job function* is a collection of tasks or units of work that are conducted by the employee that produce a result. These are the fundamental job duties and include both essential and nonessential job duties. Often, job descriptions and job functions are created before the *job focus* is considered. Job focus (which is often a missing part of the job description) can be referred to as the expectation statement. Failure to understand the job focus creates ambiguity and inconsistency across the organization.

Preparing a Results-Oriented Job Description

There are seven elements in the results-oriented job description:

- job detail
- purpose statement
- principal accountabilities
- competency
- job function (essentials and nonessentials)
- performance measures
- organizational chart

Table 7.1   Example of Job Details

Department:	Discharge Planning Department	**Dept. No.:**	P727
Job title:	RN Care Coordinator	**Status:**	Exempt
Reports to:	Manager, Discharge Planning Department	**Date:**	Jan. 1, 2008

Table 7.2   Example of Purpose Statement

Action verb: *What is done?*	Object: *For whom or what?*	Result: *For what outcome?*
To ensure appropriate services are rendered in the most appropriate healthcare setting, in an effective manner	for the patients we are privileged to serve	while supporting the mission, vision, and values of the organization as evidenced by the management of hospital costs, operations, customer service, and quality of care.

Job details include basic information about the job, such as title, direct supervisor, and department. Table 7.1 shows an example of job details.

The job description should always include a *purpose statement*. The purpose statement is often a one-sentence summary that states why the job exists. Many companies provide a small paragraph. The purpose statement should indicate the value and significance of the job and should also be as specific as possible.

Always attempt to create a purpose statement (Table 7.2) that specifically identifies:

■ What is done.
■ For whom or what is done
■ For what outcome

For example:

> To ensure appropriate services are rendered in the most appropriate healthcare setting, in an effective manner for the patients we are privileged to serve, while supporting the mission, vision, and values of the organization as evidenced by the management of hospital costs, operations, customer service, and quality of care.

The next section of the job description deals with the tasks and outcomes of the job. These may be referred to as duties, tasks, or *principal*

Table 7.3 Tasks, Stakeholders, and Purpose

What is done?	For whom or what?	To achieve what outcome?
1. Works collaboratively with members of the interdisciplinary team	on behalf of the patient, family, significant other, and physician	in an effort to facilitate discharge planning communication and a seamless patient transition to the next and most appropriate level of care.
2. Responsible for completing the initial discharge planning screen	for the patient	in an effort to identify and address patient needs.
3. Responsible for meeting	with the patient, family members, and/or significant others	to discuss potential discharge dates, plans, financial options and serve any required notices per commercial or governmental guidelines.
4. Performs admission, concurrent, and retroactive reviews	and applies various payer rules	in order to obtain authorization for the continued use of acute-care services.
5. Provides unit-based oversight	of Core Measure compliance	in an effort to communicate gaps to the bedside nurse.

accountabilities. The focus of the accountability is to achieve a specific result. Each accountability is distinct and needs to include a specific output that should be achieved by the employee. When recreating existing job descriptions or developing new ones, use brainstorming to produce the lists; take each accountability and answer what is done, for whom or what, and for what outcome. Table 7.3 illustrates this methodology.

The number of principal accountabilities should typically be between 12 and 15 for the members of discharge planning departments. Many discharge planning departments have assumed additional roles, thereby increasing the number of accountabilities.

A *competency* includes skills, attitudes, beliefs, and behaviors of a person that differentiates superior performance in a role. These are the knowledge, skills, attitudes, behaviors, and motives that will lead to high performance. Whereas the principal accountabilities represent the outcomes of a position, the competency represents the inputs of the job. The following are examples of competency:

- Must be a registered nurse from an accredited school of nursing with a minimum of three years of acute-care nursing experience.
- Must hold a current licensure as a registered nurse in the state of Ohio.
- Bachelor of Science in Nursing and previous Utilization Review/ Management and/or CDMP experience preferred.
- Strong interpersonal skills required.
- Prefer previous experience with Utilization Review/Management, Case Management, Discharge Planning, CDMP.
- Knowledge of insurance guidelines, federal regulations, and community resources preferred.

Job function includes the essential and nonessential functions of the position; the job-function list is intended to describe the general nature and level of work to be performed by the incumbent. It should not be an exhaustive list of duties. The following are examples of job-function characteristics:

- Must be able to move about the hospital and between workstations.
- Must be self-directed and take the necessary initiative to meet outcomes and targets.
- Must have excellent interpersonal skills and exercise professional behavior.

The key to a results-oriented job description is the inclusion of *performance measures*. This is the portion of the job description that shares how performance will be measured against accountability. Job descriptions that include the principal accountabilities in tandem with performance measures help create the job focus for members of the discharge planning team. Table 7.4 illustrates the inclusion of performance measures within the job description.

The addition of performance measures creates focus for the discharge planning department. As noted in Chapter 3 and Chapter 4, the performance measures must be measurable. The measure must be tied into the mission, vision, and values of the organization. Finally, the measures must be tied into the COS-Q snapshot.

The adoption of a results-oriented job description assists with creating a clear job description that also defines the job function and the job focus. When these elements are not defined, there is a lack of departmental clarity.

Finally, the job description should include a pictorial representation of where the job fits into the *organizational chart*. This should, at minimum, define who the employee reports to and identify peer members of the team. It is also helpful if the organizational chart ties back into the president or

Table 7.4   Accountability Through Performance Measures

What is done?	For whom or what?	To achieve what outcome?	Performance Measure
1. Works collaboratively with members of the interdisciplinary team	on behalf of the patient, family, significant other, and physician	in an effort to facilitate discharge planning communication and a seamless patient transition to the next and most appropriate level of care.	Facilitates interdisciplinary rounds in unit every Monday, Wednesday, and Friday.
2. Responsible for completing the initial discharge planning screen	for the patient	in an effort to identify and address patient needs.	Demonstrates 100% completion of the initial discharge planning assessment within 24 hours of admission or next business day.
3. Responsible for meeting	with the patient, family members, and/or significant others	to discuss potential discharge dates, plans, financial options and serve any required notices per commercial or governmental guidelines.	Documents one entry on every medical record that notes patient/family involvement regarding discharge planning or financial options. For Medicare, includes 100% oversight of serving the important message from Medicare (IMM) 48 hours prior to discharge.
4. Performs admission, concurrent, and retroactive reviews	and applies various payer rules	in order to obtain authorization for the continued use of acute-care services.	Must demonstrate less than 2% denials due to payer compliance issues.
5. Provides unit-based oversight	of Core Measure compliance	in an effort to communicate gaps to the bedside nurse.	Must support the Core Measure target as evidenced by tracking compliance.

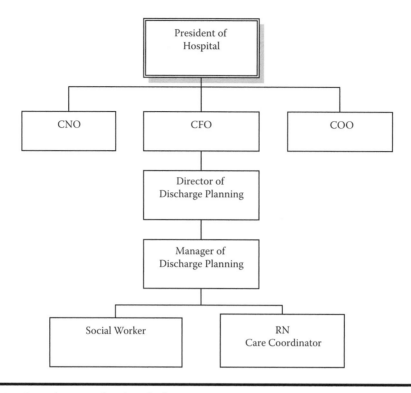

Figure 7.1   Sample organizational chart

CEO of the hospital. This provides team members with an underlying understanding of how they fit in as an employee in the company. A sample organizational chart is depicted in Figure 7.1.

Job descriptions often become outdated, so it is advantageous to review them annually with team members. This allows managers to use the job description as a tool to facilitate employee ownership and support for the position. It also reinforces the job focus and parameters that are being measured. A well-written job description also helps managers and team members make better hiring decisions, which ultimately promotes building the right team for organizational success.

Chapter 8

Interactive Discharge Planning

The opposite of proactive is reactive; the spirit of reactive people is the transfer of responsibility. Their language absolves them of responsibility.

S. R. Covey

In this chapter, readers will learn:

- differences between reactive and proactive discharge planning
- migration to interactive discharge planning
- the value of team members empowered to perform
- the need for leadership support

According to the Centers for Disease Control (CDC), hospital ALOS (average length of stay) in the 1980s was 7.3 days.[1] This allowed nurses and social workers ample time to develop and implement the discharge plan. Based on the DRG (diagnosis-related group) system, by 2005 ALOS had decreased to 4.5 days.[2] This dramatic shift in the ALOS has forced today's discharge planners to operate in an urgent environment, where the handling of multiple priorities is the norm. In an effort to meet business, quality, and customer expectations, discharge planning departments have made futile attempts to transition from reactive to proactive processes. As the scope of this function continues to expand, so does the complexity of patient and family needs. In response, discharge planners must again transform.

Reactive to Proactive

Team members that often act in response to an urgent discharge planning need or patient issue are characterized as reactive discharge planners. Tasks are generally initiated based on a trigger such as a physician order for a social work referral or post-acute-care service. In a reactive strategy, the team member knows the situation and takes any steps necessary to complete the task. Tremendous effort is required to address the impending issue because of a lack of preplanning. A common example is the late discharge on Friday that forces the discharge planner to coordinate the physician, patient, family, and administrative expectations before 5:00 p.m. In the vast majority of cases, the patient may wait until Monday morning before being discharged.

In the last ten years, many hospitals have made great strides in transitioning from reactive to proactive discharge planning strategies. Proactive discharge planning team members anticipate discharge planning needs. For example, in a proactive environment, patients over the age of 85 are automatically assessed by a social worker. In this strategy, tasks and direction are anticipated based on possible outcomes. Much of the transition was attributed to the ability of a hospital to provide more-focused strategies such as the checklist and the high-risk indicator screening. Proactive strategies have the disadvantage of overutilizing resources in an effort to avoid the risk of a last-minute discharge planning need.

Proactive to Interactive

From a discharge planning perspective, favorable outcomes have been achieved by implementing an interactive style. This strategy stipulates that discharge planners be involved and connected to the problem throughout the entire process. These members have their "fingers on the pulse" and expand their scope beyond the task of the discharge planning process. They are aware of the direction of the entire organization, not just their immediate environment. This requires a high level of insight, awareness, and communication with other ancillary functions. This approach optimizes resource utilization by balancing what is required with what is anticipated. Discharge planners today must embrace the transition from reactive to proactive and, now, to interactive strategies in an effort to manage the discharge planning process. Table 8.1 demonstrates the differences between the various strategies.

Table 8.1   Comparison of Reactive, Proactive, and Interactive Strategies

	Reactive	*Proactive*	*Interactive*
Benefit	Task is evident Must take rapid action	Head off trouble or anticipated request	Very involved with the environment Optimal decisions
Learning	Does not expand knowledge Does not expand skills Does not find a better way	Always looking forward Rarely reflects or evaluates results	High level of insight and knowledge building
Cost	Throws all resources to the situation at once	May overutilize resources when not warranted	Maximization of resources, no waiting, overplanning, or "jumping the gun"
Characterization	Coiled Anticipating Defensive Vigilant	Pushing out Busy Alert Vigilant	Involved Asking questions Doing research Finding out how things work

Source: Fritz M. Brunner,[3] "Be Interactive, Not Reactive or Proactive";
http://ezinearticles.com/?Be-interactive,-Not-Reactive-or-Proactive&id=
73519&opt=print.

When discharge planners transition to being interactive, understanding the bigger picture is the key to success. This occurs by being alert to key variables at every decision point. For example, when making clinical decisions, the interactive discharge planner balances patient rights, Core Measures, readmission, resource management, advocacy, and continuum-of-care variables. On another level, the interactive discharge planner also has to balance the needs of the physician, the organization, and the patient/family. Finally, all of these elements are put into the context of the COS-Q by balancing costs, operations, service, and quality indicators. This interactive strategy forces an optimal decision by considering all variables that may impact it (see Figure 8.1).

As team members transition to interactive styles, they must have guidance from leadership to help recognize their own personal power, knowledge, and skill sets that they contribute to the company. Because of its organic

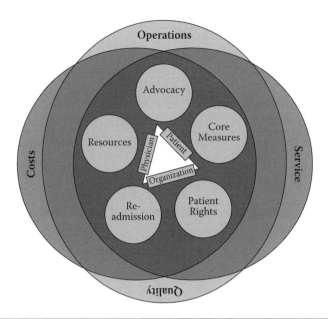

Figure 8.1 A new vision for discharge planning

nature, the staff is by default empowered to make decisions. Adopting and implementing standard criteria subsets, coupled with building processes around the outcomes the company plans to achieve, is another crucial step in the discharge planning function. Establishing guidelines on *what* dialogue to use, and *when* and *how* to use it is essential.

Empowered to Perform: Being Interactive

When it comes to discharge planning, the most successful team members are the ones who are able to convey options and solutions to patients, physicians, family members, and caregivers. They suggest or offer solutions to problems rather than merely discussing or highlighting the issue. In healthcare, patients, family members, physicians, and caregivers are constantly confronted with issues or problems with little resolve. When a discharge planner is not equipped to create solutions, physicians and others who can influence the circumstance do not consider the team member as credible. This can negatively impact the relationship that discharge planners have with ancillary members of the healthcare team.

According to authors like Covey,[4] the words we use are critical and powerful. Words have an ability to shape behavior and values. The better we are at using proactive words, the better we become at managing expectations and influencing outcomes. Proactive words lead to proactive behaviors. "A serious problem with reactive language is that it becomes a self-fulfilling prophecy".[4] Taking steps toward changing language that creates problems to language that creates solutions can have very favorable impacts on the circumstance. Building on Covey's viewpoint, we further enhance outcomes by adding an interactive style. This means adding insight into day-to-day processes and ensuring that information is communicated to all parties. In essence, this helps manage and improve the customer's expectations.

For example, compare the following reactive vs. proactive vs. interactive responses:

- ■ *Reactive*: The insurance company has issued a denial for this hospital stay.
- ■ *Proactive*: The insurance company has issued a denial, but here are some suggestions that I think might work in either getting approval to keep the patient here or facilitating a discharge while at the same time being able to meet the patient's needs.
- ■ *Interactive*: (example of a conversation that occurs one day earlier than the reactive or proactive responses) "Dr. Smith, as I reviewed Mrs. Jones's record, I noticed that, by tomorrow, she may not have enough clinical evidence to support an additional day in the hospital. I discussed the option of her going home in the event you would want to discharge her today, and she was very agreeable to this. If she is appropriate to discharge this evening, I can set up home care from our hospital for her, if she would be agreeable to that plan."

In this example, the discharge planner is managing the physician and patient expectations while demonstrating knowledge of options from the health plan and post-acute care. The team member is also attempting to control ALOS, avoid a denial, and gain an internal referral. This is called *balancing COS-Q*.

Leadership Support

Because team members are no longer in their comfort zone when transitioning to interactive processes, resistance should be expected. It requires the communication of information, learning how to position, changing the type of language used to share information, and interfacing more with other members of the healthcare team, including physicians. Not all discharge planning team members are able to make these types of adjustment.

Be prepared for what William Bridges, author of *Managing Transitions*, referred to as "the blank stares, muttering, foot-dragging, and subtle sabotage" that turns a good plan into an unworkable mess. According to Bridges,[5] "It isn't the changes that do you in, it's the transitions. Change is not the same as transition. Change is the situation: the new site, the new boss, the new team roles, and the new policy. Transition is the psychological process people go through to come to terms with the new situation. Change is external, transition is internal."

The internal process of transition is a slow one. In many discharge planning departments, transitions occur more smoothly when the change agent actually spends time connecting with team members on a daily basis. The degree to which transition is required does impact the time needed to prepare the team for transition. In most departments, change is most effective when team members participate in the planning phase and assist with communicating information back to the team. Once the transition is understood, a pilot project launched in a particular unit allows for key steps of the implementation to be "tested" and communicated back to the team members. This allows others to understand what to expect, which in turn helps them formulate their own action plans for how they will handle the transition. Communication is key. Have confidence in team members. Encourage your team with positive feedback as opposed to critical comments. Team members will learn very quickly that proactive measures increase the ability to control outcomes and manage day-to-day processes.

Team members need to feel supported as they begin to communicate issues and offer solutions to physicians, patients, family members, caregivers, and other members of the healthcare team. Staff members need to be assured that when conversations get "heated," they can count on leadership to support them. Moving the discharge planning department from a reactive to an interactive process is absolutely critical in improving COS-Q. While the transition is not always easy, the process (if facilitated smoothly) results in a team that is empowered and confident to face the challenges of the role.

References

1. Medical College of Wisconsin; www.healthlink.mcw.edu/article/1013703870.html.
2. Centers for Disease Control; www.cdc.gov/nchs/data/ad/ad385.pdf.

3. F. M. Brunner, "Be Interactive, Not Reactive or Proactive"; http://ezinearticles.com/?Be-interactive,-Not-Reactive-or-Proactive&id=73519&opt=print.
4. S. R. Covey, *The 7 Habits of Highly Effective People*. New York: Simon & Schuster, 1990.
5. W. Bridges, *Managing Transitions: Making the Most of Change* Reading, Mass.: Perseus Books, 1991.

Chapter 9

Tipping toward Technology

For new processes to be embraced, people have to believe that it has 10 times the advantage of what they were previously doing.

Peter Drucker

In this chapter, readers will learn:

- how to make the case for change
- failures of technology solutions
- solutions for technology failures
- the vendor selection process

More than 90% of all new process-transformation failures occur at execution. Experience shows that the root cause of these failures is almost always derived from two sources. First is the buy-in required from the staff to accept the new processes, and second is the ability of the organization to optimize its processes before they are automated to realize the business objectives. Lean, Six Sigma, and Action Workout methodologies assist in making change practical by making the argument for change using a disciplined approach.

There are three ingredients required for team members to embrace change. These include the *why*, *what*, and *how* of change. It is imperative that the team knows very specifically *why* change is occurring. The optimal environment for change is one in which there is no alternative. Organizations that are struggling financially are generally ready for change because the alternative is bankruptcy. When the environment is ripe for change, team members have a clear vision of *why* there must be change. Next, they need to know exactly what will change and what the new environment will look like. The *what* can be strategic in nature and does not have to be tactical in its details. *How* is the key that provides a step-by-step instruction for the transition, also referred to as *process transformation*. For this process to occur, it is important to know what the gap is between the current environment and the future vision. Once the gap has been determined, a step-by-step plan can be developed to map out the process of the transition.

Resistance to Change

Even though the environment may be right for change, people often still have a tendency to resist change. There are three main reasons why people resist: technical, political, and cultural issues. To make the transition successfully, it is imperative to manage all of these obstacles.

Technical reasons why staff fear change are derived from the fact that the new job may entail tasks that are not within the skill set of the current job description. This could include new technology or new processes. Fear of the new technical environment makes the transition seem not worthwhile. A good method to overcome technical fears is to stress the retraining and retooling that the staff will receive to transition into the new environment.

Political reasons for resistance are very common in healthcare. Large tertiary hospitals generally have over 100 major departments. These departments may reside in as many as 10 different divisions. Changes in structure may realign domains of control and power. To overcome resistance based on political issues, always keep the focus on the functions and not the divisions. The patient does not care what division is providing the service at each stage. Often called "systems thinking," in this approach individuals are minimized and the process becomes the focus.

Cultural issues are some of the toughest issues to overcome in healthcare. This form of resistance avoids change because it does not "feel right." It is very common in human nature and exists in almost all facets of human life. For example, tonight ask a spouse to sleep on the other side of the bed. Although this may seem like a meaningless change, because it just does not "feel right," there will most likely be resistance. The best way to combat cultural issues is either to start from the top by changing the way the leadership thinks and hope that it filters down to the staff, or to provide continuous communication so that it becomes part of the environment.

Table 9.1   Change Matrix

Opportunities For Change	Threats For Change	Opportunities Against Change	Threats Against Change
Arguments for Change		Arguments Against Change	

Change Matrix

There is a tool that can be utilized to assess the benefits of change called the *change matrix*. With this tool, all opportunities and threats associated with a proposed change are measured and categorized for evaluation. The process begins by bringing the stakeholders together and discussing all the reasons why change should or should not occur. The matrix quickly breaks down the reasons into arguments for and against change. Table 9.1 illustrates this matrix.

As an example, the process of formulating the arguments for or against an organization purchasing a new automated system for the care-coordination process would be as follows:

1. List the opportunities for bringing in a new automated system.
2. List the consequences of not making the change to a new automated system.
3. List the reasons why this opportunity is not as good as another opportunity.
4. List the reasons why a new automated system may threaten the business.

Based on the reasons listed in Table 9.2, it becomes evident that the arguments for change are much more compelling than the arguments against change.

Table 9.2 Change Matrix Example

Opportunities For Change	Threats For Change	Opportunities Against Change	Threats Against Change
1. Faster turnaround time 2. Better documentation 3. Automated faxing 4. Outside referrals 5. Elimination of Triple Entry 6. Automation link to insurers 7. Access to EMR	1. Competition is going automated 2. Discharges need to occur faster in order to meet budget next year 3. Patient complaints will continue to grow	1. Money could be used elsewhere	1. People may not use the system 2. System might not help the problem
Arguments for Change		*Arguments Against Change*	

Going through this process in an open environment with the staff will assist in making the case for change if the merits exist. Additionally, this will give the staff a chance to see what other colleagues think and allow the opportunity for the less vocal team members to contribute to the discussion.

Automation: The Cornerstone of Process Reengineering

In the early 1990s, the vast majority of healthcare organizations started to experience unprecedented pressures exerted by payers across the country. These payers were led by Medicare and Medicaid through cost-reduction measures designed to keep escalating double-digit healthcare increases in check. In this new, rapidly changing environment, many hospitals looked at automation as the "silver bullet" that would modernize operations to realize efficiencies and ultimately become more effective.

Unfortunately, technology in healthcare was (and is still today) relatively new. Most products are still not integrated and often are unable to produce a number for ROI (return on investment). Other setbacks were based on technology implementation methodologies that resulted in highly publicized disasters. For example, a large integrated delivery system in California implemented a very costly EMR (electronic medical record) solution, only to abandon it in the ensuing years. These setbacks were a function of basic change-enablement methodologies that included the following:

1. *No existing benchmarks for large-scale process automation in healthcare*: Since most technologies were new, there was nothing to measure against.
2. *Lack of experienced project managers*: The vast majority of experienced project managers came from the ranks with little to no experience in managing large-scale projects. PMI (Project Management Institute) was relatively new, so no governing body even existed to help train for best practices.
3. *Ineffective connection between the business and technology drivers*: Many organizations found themselves implementing technologies without understanding the operational outcome. Others experienced a flawless go-live, but with little to no benefit for the business. Hence departments often absorbed staggering annual maintenance costs but gained very little in benefits.
4. *Going from conception to implementation directly with no up-front analysis*: By far, this has been the largest driver of poor outcomes in technology implementation. By not analyzing the operational processes up front, the project almost always fails to produce the expected benefits.
5. *Automating poor processes*: Because the measure of success for the organization is different than the measure of success for the technology vendors, it is not surprising that many poor processes become automated. Hence the organization finds itself with the same poor process that produced errors, but now coming at a faster rate.

Most healthcare organizations have been transitioning toward a more stable and measurable process that takes operations into account from a systems perspective. "Systems" is defined as all relative components, including people, processes, and technology. It is imperative that all departments within the enterprise, including the discharge planning department, optimize the existing processes before automating.

Today, most project managers in large-scale healthcare projects are led by process engineers, usually with an industrial engineering background, and often with Six Sigma Black Belt certification. This did not happen by accident, but rather was the outcome of a painful and expensive process that our predecessors went through in the last two decades. Before automating any process, it is imperative that the discharge planning department leadership, along with process engineers, document, analyze, and optimize the existing processes.

The tools that can be used for this process begin with evaluating work flow. In this process, the work flow is mapped out with pertinent information about each process. Tasks that are manual vs. automated are noted.

Other pieces of information such as volumes, technology vendors, people, and security accesses are also noted during the work-flow documentation process. Once this information is compiled, areas of opportunity are noted.

1. Can any tasks be automated?
2. Can any tasks be eliminated?
3. Can any tasks be consolidated?
4. What are the points of weakness for quality and service?
5. Where are the bottlenecks occurring?

Once these opportunities for change are documented, more information must be gathered about the identified tasks for final design changes. The team at this point can design the process to meet the vision of leadership and the requirements of the business. This process ultimately develops a blueprint for the department and a guideline for the staff to improve weak points, and is also a resource for the technology vendor at the kickoff of system configuration. This documentation is critical in the discharge planning process, since the amount of interaction between people, processes, and technology across the continuum of care is significant.

For example, there are floor nurses, case managers, discharge planners, medical doctors, midlevel providers, ancillary staff members, utilization-review nurses, and social workers who interact during the course of each patient's stay. Making sure that the impact of various changes through new technology is accounted for is not just good common sense, it is critical to a successful transformation.

Gap Analysis

Once work flow is completed, analyzed, and redesigned based on the business requirements, a gap analysis must be performed. In this process, both the future and current state are placed next to each other and evaluated for differences. These differences are documented and categorized into various groups either by function or by sequence. The gap analysis is critical because it is the basis for knowing what has to be completed in order to make a successful transition to the new process. This is essential for the project manager to understand in order to educate the department and the organization as to what will occur. Additionally, the vendor will have a concrete understanding of how it must configure the system.

Organizations that are unprepared for system design in a vacuum of information will suffer the consequences of optimizing the processes after go-live. Most vendors spend very few days configuring the system with management, operating under the assumption that the team has a good feel for the future processes. Although best practices may be provided, it is risky to implement changes that have not been evaluated by the team first. Often in discharge planning design sessions, current processes are automated, and inherent processes flaws are hardwired into the system.

There are two approaches in technology-adoption strategies. First is the "vanilla" approach, and second is the "blue sky" approach. In the vanilla model, the premise is similar to a "one size fits all" approach, where the technology is based on best practices. By adopting the process standard in the system with minimal adjustment, the staff by default would be utilizing best practices. The advantage of this approach is that implementation costs are reduced almost by half and little visioning is required, since the future processes are predetermined by the system. The disadvantage of this approach is that it limits adaptation of the system to nuances of the specific environment. For example, there are regulations that are state specific and may require software to document fields that other states may not require.

The "blue sky" approach reengineers the department functions solely based on business requirements and is absent of any limitations. In this approach, all processes are optimized before the system is implemented. The technology is considered supplemental to the new departmental processes. The advantage of this approach is that it strives to achieve an optimal state of operations. The disadvantage is that most systems in the healthcare sector today do not have the capability to adapt all the permutations of each environment.

Technology Vendor Selection Process

As an increasing number of hospitals transform their operations to meet the challenges of the future, process automation is almost always the cornerstone of that change. As discussed in Chapter 2, discharge planning functions lend themselves to automated processes based on the volumes of paperwork, staff movement, and documentation. Once a decision is made to bring in new technology, it is the responsibility of the stakeholders to make sure that the right system is purchased and implemented in the most efficient manner. The foundation for an ideal vendor selection is to use a systematic process that builds on each decision point. There are 10 steps to a systematic vendor selection process:

1. *Formulate the right team*: A solid vendor-selection process begins by making sure the right people are at the table from the beginning. This means not only looking at internal stakeholders, but also at external stakeholders that could potentially derail the project if their business requirements are not met. Most critical is the participation of the nursing and physician components for discharge planning systems.

2. *Compile the business requirements*: All good vendor selection processes begin with knowing the requirements for the automation technology. This step starts with identification of all gaps between the current and future state. These gaps are turned into optional requirements.

3. *Create a selection criterion*: A good model for comparing and ranking proposals from the different vendors is based on a weighted scale. It begins with a list of criteria in five general categories: vendor experience, technical, operational, implementation, and support metrics.

   – *Vendor experience*: This section queries vendors for their experience, development, and strategic direction.

   – *Technical*: This section is generally developed by the technology department and queries the vendor's product based on the hardware and software.

   – *Operational*: This criterion refers to the flow of the software and the ease of navigation for the users. It includes the number of screens utilized to complete a process, as well as the integration required to prevent the user from leaving the system or the desk.

   – *Implementation*: This section queries vendors for information on the number of installs, implementation failures, and live sites. A good indicator to measure a vendor commitment to installs is the ratio of sales to implementation staff.

   – *Support*: This section evaluates the vendor support systems. It is critical to understand questions such as problem response time and escalation processes. Internally, it is important to make sure that there is a clear distinction between expectation of the internal technical staff, the vendor, and the department superusers.

     The team should differentiate between its "wish list" and the "deal breakers" on this list. The list of criteria can become very extensive based on the business study conducted. In some cases, organizations that are familiar with technology opt to create the criterion list based on the top 20 functions that differentiate vendors from one another. This model requires an extensive knowledge of the vendor products and existing departmental processes.

4. *Create vendor long list*: After the requirements are gathered and the criteria set, the team must begin compilation of all vendors that provide the desired technology. The only reason to eliminate specific vendors at this point should be based on strategic reasons. Resources for learning about existing vendors include searching the Web, reading trade magazines, talking to other companies, and going to conferences. The purpose of this step is to gather a comprehensive list of vendors to consider further and to assist in identifying unknown potential candidates.

5. *Create vendor short list*: Perform an initial, high-level evaluation of the long list, looking for obvious reasons to eliminate some of the alternatives. The purpose of this step is to create a short list of potential vendors that, based on the team consensus, have the best chance of potentially meeting the selection criteria.

6. *Schedule vendor demos*: Not all end-users have seen or heard of the various products, so it is critical to have the vendors bring the product to them. Through vendor demos, the end-users get a chance to "test drive" and learn about the navigation of the system. It is important to create a feedback mechanism to capture the advantages and disadvantages of the systems from all front-line employees.

7. *Submit request for proposal (RFP)*: The RFP process is the formal request from a vendor to provide a proposal based on the criteria provided. This document should begin by communicating the contact information and the deadline for response. The next section should include background on the organization(s) and the reasons that have precipitated this initiative. The third section generally includes the entire list of criteria. The last section of the RFP generally includes a financial template. This is critical, because the vendors may exclude or recategorize costs into other sections. The template forces each vendor to categorize costs in a standard way in order to make it easier for an apples-to-apples comparison when the responses are returned.

8. *Evaluate vendor proposals*: This can be the most difficult part of the vendor selection process. Vendor capabilities must be mapped against your requirements and weighting factors to determine which vendor most closely meets the needs of the organization. You can also request to interview the vendors and visit the vendor's site. Usually, some type of numerical calculation will be made based on how well the vendor

meets each requirement, multiplied by a weighting factor. The vendor with the highest score across all requirements should be the one that best meets the organization's needs. This final step provides the team with a prioritized list.

9. *Schedule site visits*: The purpose of the site visit is to verify the information provided by the vendor in the RFP. In some cases, the organization may complete a site visit prior to receiving the proposal. This includes cases where a single vendor of choice has been selected.

10. *Final selection and contract negotiation*: In many organizations, the project team makes the final recommendation and presents the information to the contracting or purchasing department for vendor negotiations. Once a final decision has been made, negotiations generally begin using boilerplate contracts. It is critical for the team to be involved in the contracting process to makes sure that the vendor response to the RFP matches the language of the contract.

In selecting a technology vendor, it is critical to align the organization's strategy to the IT department's strategy and the discharge planning business strategy. For example, if the strategic direction of the organization is to reduce costs to stay profitable, and the IT department determines that this can be achieved by going to a single database, it is incumbent on the discharge planning department to create a short list of vendors who can operate within those parameters. A good point of interaction between the various divisions in determining strategic alignment is when determining "wants" vs. "needs."

Change is about people, and it needs to begin before the introduction of new technologies. It starts by creating an environment that is conducive to new innovations. This process will always begin with the staff and often end with new processes and technologies. It is critical to use change-enablement tools to show the staff the benefits of a new vision and help answer the *what, how,* and *why* of change to minimize resistance. Once the staff is on board, the team needs to take the future vision and create processes that meet those business needs. This step prevents the department from automating bad processes. It is important to recognize that the technology is only the tool. When selecting this tool, it is critical to create a systematic process so that each decision can build upon previous decisions.

Chapter 10

Six Sigma Simplified

Every new body of discovery is mathematical in form because there is no other guidance we can have.

Charles Darwin

In this chapter, readers will learn:

- the history of Six Sigma
- the principles of Six Sigma
- the DMAIC model
- common Six Sigma tools
- the basics of a normal distribution curve
- a Lean–Six Sigma Action Workout (a practical approach)

Since 2000, a new methodology for performance improvement called Six Sigma has been sweeping healthcare organizations across the country. Early results from hospitals that implemented changes using this tool show great promise for the future. Although this methodology is statistical in nature, many discharge planning departments have adopted a more practical version called the Action Workout to implement change. This chapter provides a high-level review of Six Sigma methodology and tools.

Six Sigma is a highly disciplined data-driven approach for improving quality. It is a business philosophy focusing on elimination of defects by reducing variability. Process variability eats away at quality, resources, and service. Additionally, Six Sigma provides a framework for managing business strategy by developing a culture of change.

Table 10.1   Defects at Each Sigma Level

% Defect Free	Defects per Million	Sigma Level
99.99966	3.4	6
99.98	233	5
99.4	6,210	4
93.3	66,807	3
69.1	308,538	2
30.9	691,462	1

The measure used to quantify defects in a system is called Sigma. The higher the Sigma, the fewer defects within a system. For example, One Sigma is a system that operates at a 30% defect-free rate, while Six Sigma systems operate at a 99.999% defect-free rate (Table 10.1). A good example of companies that operate in the 6–10 Sigma ranges are the airlines. By contrast, the IRS operates at One Sigma, which accounts for the high error rates in this industry.

One common standard that is used to calculate the number of defects in a system is called defects per million opportunities, or DPMO. This number measures the defects allowed per million parts. Six Sigma processes are virtually defect-free, since only 3.4 defects are allowed per million opportunities. Most companies operate at Four Sigma, which allows 6,000 defects per million operations in a process. Discharge planning is estimated to be at approximately Two Sigma. Errors can be defined as late discharges, missed rounds, late placements in post-acute care, concurrent patient reviews, etc. Table 10.1 is a grid that helps explain defects at each Sigma level.

Six Sigma began in the 1980s, when Motorola set out to reduce the number of defects in its own products. Motorola identified ways to cut waste, improve quality, reduce costs, and focus on how the products were designed and made. Six Sigma grew from proactive thinking to the use of exact measurements and the anticipation of problem areas. In 1988, Motorola was selected as the first large manufacturing company to win the Malcolm Baldridge National Quality Award. Today, many healthcare companies are betting that the Six Sigma methodology is the "silver bullet" that will provide the edge to help them survive in these tumultuous times.

Figure 10.1   Six Sigma DMAIC Model

The DMAIC Model

The Six Sigma methodology is based on the DMAIC model (define, measure, analyze, improve, and control shown in Figure 10.1). These five steps break down the performance improvement (PI) process into five distinct structured phases that are extremely data driven.

1. *Define, identify, prioritize, and select the right projects.* In this step of the process, it is critical that the project be clearly defined and articulated. In the Six Sigma approach, it is imperative that the problem be both concise and measurable. Stay away from objectives that are broad or hard to measure. Common tools used to help define problems and objectives include "the 5 Whys." In this process, the team asks *why* five times in order to dig deeper beyond the symptoms and into the root cause of the problem.

2. *Measure the key product characteristics and process parameters.* In this step, the basic metrics are identified and gathered for analysis. Critical measures that are necessary to evaluate the success of the project are identified and determined. The initial capability and stability of the project is determined in order to establish a measurement baseline. Valid and reliable metrics to monitor the progress of the project are established during the measure phase. Input, process, and output indicators are identified. Once the project has a clear definition with a clearly measurable set of indicators, the process is studied to determine

the key process steps and develop an operational plan defined to measure the indicators. Key inputs are prioritized to establish a short list to study in more detail and to determine the potential ways the process could go wrong. Once the reasons for input failure are determined, preventive action plans are put into place.

3. *Analyze and identify the key process determinants.* In the analysis phase, the captured data is analyzed for trends and opportunities. Through the analysis phase, the team can determine the causes of the problem that need improvement and how to eliminate the gap between existing performance and the desired level of performance. This involves discovering why defects are generated by identifying the key variables that are most likely to create process variation. As the Six Sigma team moves through the analysis and subsequent improvement stage, they will discover various process-improvement scenarios and determine which has the best net benefit for the company. A common error people make when they discuss Six Sigma is thinking that the DMAIC process takes too long to achieve improvements. This is far from the truth. Quick improvements are often achieved early in the project and are frequently already implemented by the time the team reaches the analysis phase. If the team has not already identified major improvements, then the breakthrough often results from careful process analysis with data. Six Sigma analysis techniques are valuable tools to uncover more difficult solutions.

4. *Improve and optimize performance.* The improvement phase is where the process transitions into solutions. Critical inputs have been verified and optimized to identify the problem causes. Once problem causes are determined in the analysis phase, the team finds, evaluates, and selects creative new improvement solutions. The team identifies and quantifies what will happen if needed improvements are not made and what will happen if the improvements take too long. This develops a cost/benefit analysis. More often than not, simple process experimentation and simulation bring the team big gains in this step. In this improvement stage, the team also develops an implementation plan with a change-management approach that will assist the organization in implementing and adapting to the solutions and the changes that will result from them. Improvements should be validated using statistical methods.

5. *Control to hold the gains.* Success in the control phase depends upon how well the team performed in the previous four phases. The keys to

success are a solid monitoring plan with proper change-management methods that identify key stakeholders. Lessons learned are now implemented and tools are put in place to ensure that the key variables remain within the acceptable ranges over time so that process-improvement gains are maintained. The team develops a project hand-off process, reaction plans, and training materials to guarantee performance and long-term project savings. Documenting the project is very important so that the new procedures and lessons learned are maintained and provide concrete examples for the organization. At the close of the control phase, ownership and knowledge is transferred to the process owner and process team tasked with the responsibilities. Finally, the team identifies what the next steps are for future Six Sigma process-improvement opportunities by identifying replication and standardization opportunities and plans.

The Pillars of Six Sigma

There are six key concepts that are often referred to as the pillars of Six Sigma. These concepts guide the methodology through the entire process from defining the problem to control in the new environment. A thorough understanding of these concepts will provide team members with the mental infrastructure required to implement a successful Six Sigma initiative.

1. *Critical to quality (CTQ)*: Attributes most important to the customer. Moreover, in measuring CTQ attributes, sensitivity analysis performed through a valid simulation is an excellent methodology for identifying the most appropriate CTQ impacting the process under review. This can usually be done more quickly and economically than using high-power statistical tools like Design of Experiments.

    An example in discharge planning is identifying the attributes that are most critical for patients in determining where they go for post-acute-care services. For large integrated delivery systems, this is very important because there is a direct relationship between profits and the reasons why patients go to the competition. Identifying the elements that control these patient patterns in discharge planning will help show variables that are critical to quality for these patients.

2. *Defect*: Failing to deliver what the customer wants. A defect in healthcare could be any outcome that was unintended. Defects cost the organization in labor, materials, and time.

An example of a defect in discharge planning is missing the discharge date.

3. *Process capability*: What your process can deliver. Having a good handle on what your processes can deliver is extremely important because it helps troubleshoot today and plan for the future.

An example in discharge planning is knowing how many patients a nurse can see per day. Knowing the process capability will allow management to forecast the impact of a change in patient patterns or an introduction of a new variable into the system.

4. *Variation*: What the customer sees and feels. Since healthcare is so local, patients rarely get the same treatment from a different provider. This variation is inherent in the fact that there is no national standard of care that is enforced.

An example of variation in discharge planning today is the discharge time of the patients on any given day. The variation in the events that establish the discharge time for a patient is so variable that it is hard to predict the discharge time with any degree of certainty. Hence, organizations that have been able to reduce this variation in the discharge process experience high patient satisfaction and increased throughput.

5. *Stable operations*: Ensuring consistent, predictable processes to improve what the customer sees and feels. People, processes, and technology must come together to ensure consistent, predictable processes. The most difficult issues to resolve in a system are those that are unpredictable.

An example of stable operations in discharge planning is the utilization of "hospitalists" (hospital-owned physicians that facilitate patients during their inpatient stay) to control the often unpredictable physician-care and discharge patterns.

6. *Design for Six Sigma (DFSS)*: Designing to meet customer needs and process capability. DFSS is an analysis technique to determine the

extent to which uncertainties in the model affect the results of an analysis. Design for Six Sigma enables users to quantify the quality of the product, addressing issues such as minimizing warranty costs and quantifying reliability. Design for Six Sigma goes one step further than a probabilistic characterization by allowing users to optimize design variables to achieve a particular probabilistic level, such as Six Sigma (i.e., 3.4 failures in 1 million parts).

> For example, different discharge planning models exist for social workers, case managers, and the utilization-review nurses. These models are based on a dyad or triad model. In DFSS, each model would be tested to see which system has the optimal balance between quality and cost.

Statistical Tools

The Six Sigma DMAIC methodology requires a significant amount of assessment using statistical tools to measure processes. Some key concepts that will help managers understand commonly used statistical terms are as follows:

■ *Control charts*: Graphs used to study how a process changes historically over time. A control chart always has a central line for the average, an upper line for the upper control limit, and a lower line for the lower control limit. By comparing points on the graph against the lines, processes can be consistent (in control) or unpredictable (out of control, affected by special causes of variation).
■ *Statistically significant*: On the average, the likelihood of an event occurring is more than by chance alone. When doing assessments of the discharge planning function, it is important to be sure the data do not lead to a conclusion based on chance.
■ *Min/Max/Avg/Med*: Minimum, Maximum, Average, and Median—basic statistical metrics that provide a quick picture of the data set. For example, in measuring staff productivity in discharge planning using cases per day, managers often use the average as the target for the staff that consistently performs at the minimum level.

When collecting data for analysis, it is important to be sure that the sample collected accurately represents the process. There are three factors

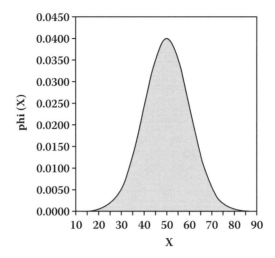

Figure 10.2   Bell-shaped curve for a normal distribution with a mean of 50 and a standard deviation of 10

that measure the viability of the sample size: confidence level, method, and duration. Confidence level is a function of test time or sample size, where the bigger the sample, the higher the confidence level. Method and duration refer to other aspects such as ensuring that data is collected at the correct intervals. This is especially important in discharge planning, since there is a tremendous amount of seasonal variation in the flow of patients for most organizations.

The normal bell distribution is a pattern for the distribution of a set of data that follows a bell-shaped curve. This distribution is sometimes called the Gaussian distribution, in honor of Carl Friedrich Gauss, a famous mathematician. The bell-shaped curve has several properties:

■ The curve is concentrated in the center and decreases on either side. This means that the data has less of a tendency to produce unusually extreme values compared with some other distributions.
■ The curve is symmetric, which means that the probability of deviations from the mean are comparable in either direction.

The probability of a variable is defined by describing the area of the bell curve. A large area implies a large probability, and a small area implies a small probability. The relationship between probability and area is also useful because it provides a visual interpretation for probability. Figure 10.2

is an example of a bell-shaped curve. This curve represents a normal distribution with a mean of 50 and a standard deviation of 10.

The Lean–Six Sigma Action Workout: Speed, Simplicity, and Strength

Buy-in from staff into the Six Sigma process is critical in changing the culture of the organization. In the past, many Six Sigma initiatives have failed because the staff found the methodology too complex or impractical. For this reason, a simplified version of Six Sigma, called Action Workout, has been developed to introduce a more practical application of the DMAIC model. In this book, the Action Workout has been modified to include Lean concepts, making the process a *Lean–Six Sigma Action Workout*.

In this process, the Six Sigma DMAIC model is used to create a disciplined approach, Lean is used to design new solutions, and Action Workout is used to make the process quick and practical. This strategy will ensure staff buy-in early in the process and sets the groundwork for quick results. Once a Lean–Six Sigma Action Workout has been implemented successfully in discharge planning, most managers and supervisors pick up on the process quickly and are able to replicate it across other units. This process has been very successful for organizations that require quick turnaround of projects and are in short supply of Six Sigma Black Belts. There are three key characteristics of a Lean–Six Sigma Action Workout:

1. *Speed*: Most Six Sigma projects are six months in duration, but Action Workouts can be completed as quickly as two months.
2. *Simplicity*: Solutions are based on staff input, visual observation of the process, and basic input/output variables. Most of the data collection and analysis is for developing baseline metrics.
3. *Strength*: By empowering the staff to analyze and develop solutions, the project gathers strength through staff buy-in.

There are generally four possible sources from which most opportunities precipitate in discharge planning. These include waste identified in existing departmental metrics, external benchmarking indicators that show outliers, novel ideas from staff, and the traditional customer complaints. In this case, the customer can be defined as the stakeholder in the process, which can include at minimum the physician and the patient.

Once the opportunity has been identified, a team is put together with as many staff members as possible. Additionally, front-line employees from departments that immediately precede and succeed the unit are also brought in. By including these stakeholders in the process, the impact of any potential changes are immediately evaluated for downstream effects. Making sure that the right staff is involved in the process ensures that there are plenty of ideas being generated and ensures better buy-in.

After the team has been brought together, it is time to define the problem statement from the opportunity. A common method used to nail down the problem is referred to as "the 5 Whys." The team continuously asks "why" five times, each time getting deeper and deeper into the root of the problem. This exercise forces the team to address the root cause vs. symptoms of the problem. Once the problem has been identified, the goals are outlined and the scope is defined in detail.

The next step in the Action Workout is to begin taking baseline metrics. Often, before measurement begins, a workflow map of the process is completed to identify critical points. Once the process steps have been identified, basic metrics are captured to illustrate the flow of inputs and outputs into the process. An example of a task's input and output in discharge planning is when data is taken from the chart (input) and put into the utilization-review "review form" (output). Most organizations begin with existing data, although sometimes it may be necessary to manually collect it. Once the workflow is complete and the metrics have been gathered, it is important to lock in the baseline metrics. These are the numbers that will be used to measure success.

The next step in the process is to analyze the data. In this step, the data is reviewed for anomalies. Quick and easy information to look for includes: up/down trends and minimum and maximum ranges. Once the data has been analyzed, it is important to try and identify the root cause of the problem. Often, the metrics used at the beginning of the process are changed during the analysis stage as new data reveal root causes that may have been identified in an unsuspected area of the process. During the analysis phase, the staff is encouraged to use Lean thinking concepts to generate ideas. A cornerstone of the Action Workout methodology is the free flow of ideas from the staff to solve root causes. To make this process easier for staff members, many facilitators utilize Post-It notes on which

Table 10.2 Grid for Treatment of Ideas

Difficulty	High difficulty Low benefit	High difficulty High benefit
	Low difficulty Low benefit	Low difficulty High benefit
		Benefit

each person writes his or her suggestions in silence. This prevents other employees from shooting down ideas during the brainstorming session.

Once these ideas have been gathered, a four quadrant grid is created on the board that measures ideas that have the most impact and those that are the most difficult to implement. Table 10.2 illustrates the four quadrants. Each suggestion on the Post-It notes are evaluated through the facilitator by the team and assigned to a quadrant. The hope is that some of the suggestions will fall into the quadrant that (1) has the most impact and (2) presents little difficulty to implement. Suggestions that are the easiest to implement and with the biggest impact are assigned "on the fly" to staff members for implementation. Each week the facilitator asks the staff for feedback on the process, and a date is determined to remeasure baseline metrics to assess progress. At the end of this process, it is imperative that the team celebrate any successes they may have realized.

Although Six Sigma is a very powerful tool for quality improvement, the Action Workout is much more practical in nature. Combined with Lean thinking, the Action Workout methodology becomes a powerful tool for change based on its practicality. Discharge planning functions can benefit tremendously from this practical approach in implementing change. The following is an actual Lean–Six Sigma Action Workout discharge planning project that was implemented in a multihospital organization.

- *The smoking gun*: The process started through a meeting that reviewed Thomson's Action O-I benchmarking data indicating labor utilization at 20% above the targets developed in the compare group. A project charter was put together with the executive sponsor and the project lead to create a mandate for change. This project was communicated to the staff.

■ *Team formulation*: The project manager selected a group of staff members from all functions in the discharge planning function across all facilities. It started with volunteers, although some assignments were made in departments that did not have representation. A bedside nurse and a process engineer were included to help with the solution analysis and development. (Tip: Try and find the most progressive staff whenever possible. Also, be sure to include new staff members. They often come in from other organizations that may have better processes or may have a different perspective.)

■ *Define*: The team defined the project by starting with the symptoms. Benchmarking data indicated that labor utilization is higher than normal for the department. The question is, why? The managers indicated a high utilization of overtime. Again, the question was asked, "Why?" Staff needs more time to manage the workload that has been developed for their targets. Again, "why" do they need more time than other organizations? Department protocols and processes are inconsistent across departments and organizations. At this point, the problem was specific enough to move forward. All organizations were to be included in the process for the scope, and a target of 10% improvement in labor productivity was set. (Tip: Be sure to constantly ask, "Why?" The more specific the problem, the easier it is to manage.)

■ *Measure*: The team put together a process workflow and provided some data associated with the volumes for each task. All inputs and outputs were noted per task. Steps that added value and those that did not were identified for review by the team. A key indicator was based on an engineering study that asked each staff member to track the number of cases per day for a two-week period. This included cases closed, cases opened, new cases, and existing cases. (Tip: It is imperative to see the process in motion when conducting a workflow. If the workflow is completed in a conference room with the manager, the ideal process may be documented instead of the actual process.)

■ *Analyze*: The data indicated that there was high variability in the number of cases being done for the same type of patients by staff between organizations and departments. This data was shared with the staff for a brainstorming session. Using Lean techniques, the staff was encouraged to look for steps that did not add value to the process. Looking at the workflow, staff members noted that the variability was derived from excessive documentation, delays in preparing the folders for the day, and the travel time between patients on floors. Using a red marker, the steps that were questionable in the process were circled as opportunities. (Tip: Try to use a facilitator that is not familiar with the process. This forces the team to ask basic questions that may not occur to staff involved day-to-day in the process.)

- *Improve*: The staff brainstormed ideas that were put on Post-It notes. Once collected, they were read aloud and put into a quadrant field based on feedback from the group. The suggestions that were in the *high-impact, low-cost* quadrant were taken off the sheet and listed in an Excel file. The director asked for volunteers from the group to take on the change implementation. A date of two weeks was selected for review of progress based on the assigned pilots. (Tip: Be sure that staff members are not allowed to judge suggestions during the brainstorming session. Everything needs to be recorded and documented.)

- *Control*: Each week, the implementation staff provided updates on the progress, which was shared with the staff. After one month the data was remeasured to evaluate progress against the baseline metrics. Best practices were shared among staff, and changes were made on an ongoing basis. The standardized-documentation approach increased the caseload for more than 25% of the staff by over 10%. (Tip: A good part of every program is to celebrate wins when there is a success. In this case, the staff had lunch catered for an entire week.)

Six Sigma is a performance improvement methodology that puts great emphasis on operating at near perfection through metrics and statistical controls. Although it is very new in healthcare, its impact has been tremendous in the manufacturing sector. Because the methodology is statistically intensive, many clinical departments in healthcare often use a variation called the Action Workout. This methodology is often interlaced with Lean thinking to create a powerful new tool called The Lean–Six Sigma Action Workout. In this process, the staff has buy-in by default, since they generate the solutions. Additionally, Lean concepts are used during the Analyze phase to provide the staff with some guidelines in identifying waste for elimination. This combination creates a powerful tool by combining the best aspects of each tool in a practical application.

Chapter 11

Creating a Culture
of Accountability

---

*A good coach will hold the team accountable for both their actions
and their results.*

Catherine Pulsifer
from Good-Bye Manager, Hello Coach!

In this chapter, readers will learn:

- how to identify lost accountability
- the definition of accountability
- strategies for gaining systems accountability
- strategies for gaining a culture of team accountability
- examples for maintaining accountability

It is easy to identify the havoc that results in an organization when
there is little to no accountability. What is more difficult to identify are the
key elements or employees needed to have a highly empowered, responsible, and enthusiastic team. Do motivated, enthusiastic, and empowered
employees exist? If so, where do they come from or how are they created?

A new administrative team member reflected on her experience: She had
visited an inner company facility where a seasoned administrator worked. The
new administrator was astonished at what she witnessed. The facility was
in tip-top shape, the employees were all smiling, helpful, and kind. They

had obvious pride in themselves and their work. The new administrator concluded that it must be nice to be able to recruit committed employees.

What the new administrator did not see was all the work and diligence of the seasoned administrator. The administrator had developed work teams. The teams were utilized to create a list of expectations that were required of the entire team. When employees met expectations, they were rewarded. Conversely, when they did not meet expectations, it was immediately addressed. The administrator met with the each employee for a face-to-face meeting periodically, often discussing things that she herself could do to help the employee perform at a more optimal level. Key to her success was creating a climate of concern for the employee, as well as a safe arena for dialogue. She took the time to reeducate her employees about expectations and offered retraining as needed. When efforts to bring an employee into compliance failed, she proceeded with due diligence and placed the employee in positive discipline. This seasoned administrator realized that if even one employee did not perform at the expected level, it impacted everyone on the team. Her careful approach demonstrated integrity, commitment and responsibility. If she elected to terminate an employee, she did so in a respectful manner. She also realized that, as a leader, she was accountable to her team. She had a process in place to ensure that her team understood expectations, and she treated her employees fairly and addressed issues instantly.

There was no real magic here, except the magic of leadership, diligence, integrity, and *accountability*. Creating an environment where accountability is embraced and where the bidirectional flow of accountability and responsibility move from leader to employee and employee to leader can often be one of leadership's greatest challenges.

Identifying Lost Accountability

Many leaders are familiar with a popular story that helps depict the errors new leaders make when attempting to transfer accountability and empowerment to their team members:

> There were once four brothers: Everyone, Someone, Anyone, and No one. They had a very important task to do. Everyone was sure that Someone would do it. Anyone could have done it, but in the end No one did it. Someone was angry because it should have

been Everyone's job. Everyone thought that Anyone could have done it, but No one realized that ultimately No one would do it. In the end, Everyone was angry at Someone because No one did what Anyone could have done.

Hospitals have struggled with creating clear expectations for members of the discharge planning team. This has resulted in a culture of employees who may lack ownership or accountability. Departments that have little to no accountability will be full of excuses for not meeting objectives. Team members may be exhibiting an undertone of apathy, or little to no real desire to do more than the minimal amount necessary. These departments display behaviors that suggest being close to the target is good enough. They often request low or ambiguous targets in an effort to produce minimal efforts.

From a discharge planning perspective, lost accountability can lead to increased lengths of stay for patients, increased denials, low rates of reimbursement for diagnosis-related group (DRGs), poor Core Measure compliance, and patient/family dissatisfaction. The unfavorable impact on the COS-Q (cost, operations, service, and quality of care) can be exponential.

Credible employees that are working in environments of low accountability quickly recognize that leadership is lacking. When departments are allowed to perform poorly, most credible employees resign from their positions. This further exacerbates a leader's ability to build effective teams committed to achieving outcomes.

What Is Accountability?

Accountability is the acknowledgement and assumption of responsibility for actions, products, decisions, and policies. This includes administration, governance, and implementation within the scope of the role or employment position, and encompasses the obligation to report, explain, and be able to answer for resulting consequences.[1]

According to AXIS Performance Advisors, Inc., accountability is one of three interlocking components of effective empowerment. The other two components are responsibility and authority. It is the balance of responsibility, authority, and accountability that creates the platform for empowered work teams. Balance is achieved when a team has (1) a clear understanding of its responsibilities, (2) the authority to fulfill these responsibilities, and (3) the accountability for the consequences of its outcomes.[2]

Many companies struggle to ensure that team members understand departmental expectations and have the authority to complete the duties assigned. In healthcare, and specifically in discharge planning departments, there are no exceptions. The mere suggestion of transferring accountability results in resistance. Many team members will argue that they are professional and should not have to be micromanaged. While leaders want to respect individuality and professionalism, today's healthcare arena demands new levels of accountability.

There has been a growth in the need for transparency in healthcare. More and more pressure is being placed on hospitals and healthcare systems to be more accountable in their actions to society and the environment. Transparency is a broad-scale initiative enabling consumers to compare the quality and price of healthcare services. These initiatives are laying a foundation for immediate access and analysis of information about procedures, hospitals, and physician services. This stems from an effort to provide the healthcare consumer with the ability to make informed choices among doctors and hospitals. The magnitude of transparency required in the healthcare industry requires hospitals to make outcomes measures, quality scores, pricing, and satisfaction scores available for public access, thus making accountability critical at every level.

For employees and leaders, accountability is a personal promise to achieve or exceed measurable results. Accountability emphasizes a commitment to performance and creates a condition in which members can understand the system, work to find the root causes of problems, and identify actions for improvement.

In high-performance organizations, workers are individually accountable to each other and mutually accountable to their customers.[2] According to research, holding people accountable for their results has very positive effects: greater accuracy of work, better response to role obligations, more vigilant problem solving, better decision making, more cooperation with coworkers, and a higher team satisfaction—in short, higher overall performance [2]. As the healthcare industry positions itself to meet the demands of the informed consumer, failure to maintain accountability at all levels will no longer be an option.

Table 11.1 The Three Basic Principles of Accountability

Achieve Focus	*Achieve Influence*	*Achieve Consequence*
Clearly communicate Continually reinforce mission and vision Require teams to describe their purpose and outcomes that link to vision Ensure that teams complete a whole piece of work Establish clear standards Allow teams to track and analyze their own performance Encourage teams to conduct regular business-planning sessions	Allow employees to participate in shaping the organizational mission/vision Teach teams to use performance feedback as the basis for meetings and problem solving Encourage teams to analyze work practices for improvement Allow teams to act on their improvement ideas Give teams as much choice as possible Give teams as much budget authority as possible Encourage open feedback Empower teams to select members Empower team to remove nonperformers	Ensure that teams get direct and regular feedback from customers Let teams carry over savings in their budgets Abolish internal monopolies Tie rewards and compensation to team outcomes Allow teams to share in the financial success of the organization

Gaining Systems Accountability

Accountability can be strongly influenced by two aspects of an organization: its systems and its culture.[2] AXIS Performance Advisors, Inc., noted that there are three basic principles that are required to build systems for accountability (see Table 11.1 for strategies on how to achieve these basic principles):

- *Focus*: Teams members must have clear expectations.
- *Influence*: Team members must have influence over their work process as well as the members on whom they are dependent.
- *Consequences*: Team members must recognize that there should be natural and logical consequences for all actions.

Gaining a Culture of Team Accountability

Creating a culture of team accountability is a somewhat bigger challenge. This means creating a work environment that embraces core values such as integrity, honesty, and fairness. It also involves creating a safe environment for employees to speak openly about issues, and requires leaders to minimize discouragement and maximize encouragement. It asks employees and leaders to focus on solutions rather than blaming someone for the problems. AXIS Performance Advisors, Inc., has suggested the following strategies:

■ Earn the trust of coworkers—do what you say, and say what you mean.
■ Publicly own up to your mistakes and accept the natural consequences for them.
■ When mistakes or problems occur, focus on the future—steer discussions to what needs to be done, not what was done.
■ Remember that intent is not the same as performance—help people follow through on their commitments.
■ Be explicit about accountability and expectations—talk openly and preferably face-to-face about responsibilities, performance standards, deadlines, and potential consequences.
■ Be supportive—help people talk about their progress and offer help when they are stuck or unsure.

As the healthcare landscape becomes more transparent and the economic climate becomes more volatile, a renewed emphasis on accountability must be accomplished. It is not enough to achieve the target for the moment. Accountability has to become the driving force that energizes performance at every level of the organization, and specifically the discharge planning department.

Maintaining Accountability

Establishing a culture of accountability in any organization is not an easy accomplishment. It takes a commitment from every level of the organization, and consistent perseverance in pushing the accountability agenda. Leaders must maintain the basic principles of accountability (focus, influence, and consequence). The following are examples of how leaders can successfully apply these three principals of accountability:

■ *Focus*: Focus creates clarity by defining expectations in a clear and specific manner. The expectations are also linked to outcomes and include the rationale behind the change.

Table 11.2 A Clearly Defined Job Expectation with Its Associated Rationale and Resultant Outcomes

Expectation:	Every chart is reviewed every day
Outcomes:	Improved ALOS
	Reduction in denials
	Reduction in discharge delays
	Improved customer service
	Improved quality of care
Rationale:	Team agrees that this is an effective method to achieve outcomes

Example: The team has agreed that reviewing every medical record every day is critical to minimizing discharge delays, shortening ALOS, (average length of stay), and reducing denials. It also improves customer service and allows the company to promote improved quality of care (see Table 11.2).

■ *Influence*: Leaders must exercise influence over team members and help them to recognize that accountability requires listening, understanding, agreeing, and committing to achieve the target. This also includes being prepared to negotiate for outcomes when valid barriers are present.

Example: Jane's monthly audit has demonstrated that she is not meeting the policy. Today, the team leader reviews the data from yesterday and notices that Jane did not meet the standard.

Leader: "Jane, on a daily basis, each team member ensures that they have reviewed every observation case. I have just pulled yesterday's report and noticed that there were three observation cases in your area that were not reviewed."

Jane: "Yesterday I had a major family issue and needed to leave on schedule. I came in early this morning to make sure these would be addressed."

Leader: "Can I count on you getting these done today?"

Jane: "Yes, you can."

Leader: "What might we do if this happens again? Do you have an idea on how we can meet your needs and our needs at the same time? Remember, failure to review the cases in a timely manner could result in a formal coaching."

Jane: "I should have called someone to ask for help. I will do that in the future."

Leader: "That sounds great, Jane. Thanks for your commitment. I appreciate the accountability."

■ *Consequences*: Designing appropriate consequences is best when team members provide input on the consequences. Additionally, for consequences to be effective, leaders must monitor for outcomes, and they must also hold themselves just as accountable as any other team member. Further, they must also have the ability to have effective conversations with staff members when expectations are not met.

Example:
- Jane and the team committed to reviewing all observation cases by 3 p.m. on a daily basis.
- Jane failed to review three cases.
- She was immediately addressed the following morning and admitted that she did not complete the work. She stated she came in early to ensure that she would complete the tasks. She also had communicated a plan in the event she should run behind again in the future.
- The subsequent morning, the report demonstrated that Jane did not meet the expectation.
- Jane was again talked to that afternoon. The coaching was done in an office setting. A climate of concern was created. She was to participate in developing an action plan to improve her performance. Jane was educated on the next levels of positive discipline. Finally, Jane was asked to document her understanding of the conversation and the document was signed, dated, and placed in her employee file.

A sense of personal credibility, ownership, and high performance can only exist in an organization when there is a culture of accountability. Healthcare transparency and public responsibility are forcing compliance to occur at an elevated level. For companies that desire to have breakthrough performance, hospital leaders must recognize that there is no substitute for the gains that can be achieved when leaders and team members alike make the personal choice to commit and achieve.

References

1. Wikipedia, "Accountability," http://en.wikipedia.org/wiki/Accountability.
2. Axis Advisory, "The Accountability Hot Potato," http://home.pacifier.com/~axis/T6potato.html.

Chapter 12

The Final Steps to Success

Success comes before work only in the dictionary.

Anonymous

With new drivers in healthcare gathering momentum, hospitals will need to continue capitalizing on every opportunity to survive. By redefining the discharge planning function, what used to be considered a cost center can quickly turn into a new revenue pipeline. This process begins by understanding the impact of discharge planning throughout the organization.

In order to maximize the benefits from this new revenue pipeline, new metrics must be identified and tracked relentlessly. The COS-Q (cost, operations, service, and quality of care) snapshot was created as a tool to help discharge planning functions monitor all of these indicators. The COS-Q combines costs, operations, service, and quality metrics into a balanced report card that maximizes value for all stakeholders.

Managing people, processes, and technology in the COS-Q is very complex and requires innovative tools. Utilization of new performance improvement (PI) methodologies such as Lean and Six Sigma are rapidly penetrating the healthcare sector. Because these tools can be complex, a practical version called the Lean–Six Sigma Action Workout has been designed to provide healthcare staff a process without the complex statistical analysis. For rapid results, 10 secrets derived from Lean thinking tools were introduced that can quickly turn the discharge planning function into a highly effective revenue pipeline. However, before implementing these changes, it is critical to implement basic infrastructure such as standardized job descriptions and interactive processes.

The Next Steps to Success

Opportunities can only be realized by organizations that have the determination and the tools to make it happen. Due to the complexity of the discharge planning function, this transformation can be overwhelming for team members and stakeholders. For a successful implementation of these new strategies, it is critical to sequence each step in the most effective manner to capitalize on momentum. The following is a guideline to serve as a framework for the changes discussed in this book.

1. Begin with educating the team on the mission, vision, and values of the company. Describe how the strategic direction of the discharge planning function serves to promote and enhance the mission, vision, and values. This can build momentum as the team begins thinking about change. The exercise of making the argument for and against change will help management create the logic behind the effort. Staff will need to know the what, how, and why of any change before buy-in is created. This lays the departmental groundwork to begin thinking about change.

2 Using Lean and Six Sigma methodologies for dynamic performance improvement is critical. Provide an in-service to orient the team to Lean concepts. Providing team members with a Lean focus creates the foundation for the departmental approach to redesign. Develop Lean "ground rules" that will serve as the parameters for solutions. For example, all decisions must incorporate the impact on downstream and upstream processes.

3. If the function is not measured, it cannot be managed. Once the organization is ready for change, it is important to lock in the baseline metrics. The most important indicators for managing the discharge planning function should be compiled into the discharge planning COS-Q snapshot. Monitoring, trending, and evaluating the snapshot are critical.

4. Begin migration to a dyad model. All ensuing decisions, such as staffing ratios, job descriptions, and capital requirements are predicated on the type of model adopted. Develop a transition plan that will address common issues such as pay grades, union issues, cultural issues, physician issues, nursing issues, and employee competencies. This is going to be

the first big hurdle, and it is not unusual for there to be significant staff resistance.

5. Design the processes needed to implement a unit-based team configuration. As the staffing plan is developed, consider all variables that impact the productivity of the team, such as the number of beds per unit, the unit type, payer mix, and turnover. This assists with the assignment of the team members. Physician-aligned case managers will provide the most issues in this change. They have the clout with the physicians and can create significant barriers. The best approach is to set this group apart and address them at the end of the process.

6. Select the medical-necessity criteria to serve as the basis for utilization-review decisions. Determine what is currently being utilized in the hospital. Are the criteria up to date? Are team members using the criteria correctly? What criteria are the health plans using in the current market? Develop competencies and audit tools to ensure standardization and consistent application of the guidelines. Also, it is worth noting that certain technology systems have the ability to incorporate the criteria right in to the system. The value of this is that staff can now query the data or instantly know when they have met the criteria.

7. Create an escalation process to address physician practice patterns, variance trends, and delay days. Develop a tracking mechanism to communicate information to senior leadership. This process lets the staff know that they have the support of the leadership.

8. A common tool used to create a standardized, legal approach to maximizing internal referrals is "scripting." For example:

Mr. Smith, my name is Betty, and one of the best parts of my job is ensuring that my patients are completely satisfied with the discharge planning process. Is there anything that I can review with you today to ensure that we have met all of your needs? Your physician has ordered an outpatient test. While you are able to choose any place that accepts Medicare beneficiaries, I thought you might like to be aware of one of our affiliated outpatient diagnostic centers that is close to your home. If it is okay with you, I can facilitate scheduling that appointment. What date and time would work best for you and your family?

It is important to review all scripts with legal counsel and compliance officers to ensure that the script meets local and state regulations.

9. There are four components that come into play in effectively managing denials and observation conversions.

   – Open up the lines of communication between members of the discharge planning team and members of the denials and appeal team.
   – Identify the top three to five reasons for denials and conversion requests.
   – Graph outcomes on a monthly basis.
   – Communicate results to the team members.

   Ask the denial nurses to provide an in-service checklist for the staff to change processes up front as much as possible.

10. Create "the day-before discharge checklist." Be prepared for barriers when implementing the checklist.

   – The team may resist when it perceives that the time needed to review the checklist will have a negative effect on productivity. Mitigation 1: Make the case that the time required to do the checklist is less than the issues that result from rework.
   – The team may resist when it perceives that the checklist is not comprehensive. Mitigation 2: Follow the 80/20 rule for impacting outcomes. Remember that perfection is the enemy of good.

11. When implementing a Clinical Documentation Management Program (CDMP), it is critical to stress that the program requires mutual respect between the nursing and coding professionals. The success of the program requires

   – a committed team member driving the outcomes
   – a team approach toward improvement
   – monthly tracking and data sharing with the team members
   – an escalation process to assist with dispute resolution between nursing, coding, and physicians

12. Position your team to utilize the Lean–Six Sigma performance-improvement methodology for incremental growth. Invest in training

a manager to become a certified Green Belt. Incorporate a high-level Lean–Six Sigma session into the employee-orientation process. Train the managers on the practical Lean–Six Sigma Action Workout methodology. Use this tool to make incremental changes toward departmental targets on the COS-Q. Check with the Quality or the Management Engineering department for resources that can assist you in this process.

13. Maintain accountability at all levels. Start with the job descriptions. Keep the new standards clear and consistent. Regular feedback prevents surprises and provides every opportunity for success.

   - Assign a leader and hold that person accountable for dates and outcomes.
   - Report outcomes on a monthly basis at both senior and operational levels.
   - Mandate action plans for failed outcomes.

14. Celebrate successes. If the organization has reached this point, it is time to let everyone know. It is not a tenet of Six Sigma and Lean to celebrate successes, but it makes good management sense. This will motivate the staff to continue the performance improvement process.

Maintain the Gain

The journey to the future may take six months to a year to complete. Although simple process changes might be quick to implement, changing the culture or implementing new technology will take much longer. In the end, it is imperative to know that this is not a single event; it is a process. Because healthcare will continue to change into the foreseeable future, it is reasonable to expect that the metrics and solutions for today's problem will, in time, be outdated.

Case Study: Reshaping Care Delivery at Hospital "A"

On August 15, 2005, with only 12 hours left before her redesign strategy presentation, Alexis J. Simms, vice president of Integrated Care Services, reflected on the challenges of putting a successful program in place. Not only was she proposing a complete redesign of the current system, but also a cultural transition that would have a significant impact on the staff. The success or failure of her future in this organization rested on the delivery of this proposal to the executive leadership in the company.

Just six months earlier, the president of Hospital "A" had demanded a Discharge Planning Redesign project. Benchmarking data indicated an overutilization of staff members and increasing average length of stay (ALOS), denials, and readmission rates. To make matters worse, internal referrals for skilled nursing and home care were diminishing. While the team had never been under scrutiny in the past, new market pressures had surfaced, creating a tidal wave of issues.

Background

Hospital "A" is a 324-bed facility nestled in an urban area of the Midwest. There are a total of six floors with two 25-bed units on each floor. There is also a 12-bed ICU and a 12-bed telemetry unit. The hospital is part of an integrated delivery system that provides outpatient services and post-acute-care services, including home care and skilled nursing. At Hospital "A," 60% of the patients are Medicare, 30% are commercial, and the remaining 10% are self-pay or other.

A recent review of the hospital data had revealed that the case-mix index had decreased, which did not coincide with a decrease in the hospital's ALOS. Traditionally, the ALOS had averaged 4.5 days and now had surged to 5.2. The hospital was also facing constrained capacity issues. On average, one to three surgeries were canceled daily due to high census, and the average hold time in the postanesthesia-care unit (PACU) was four hours. Additionally, the emergency department was on diversion for an average of four hours per month. Emergency department patients were held in the unit for an average of six hours waiting for a bed. On average, there were 17,820 discharges per year. Bed turnover had decreased by 2%; this decrease was significantly impacting the bottom line.

Customer service was at an all-time low, and surveys revealed that continuity of care and discharge planning were below target. Physicians were also dissatisfied with poor communication, perceived poor hospital quality, and lack of coordination of services. Commercial denials were on the rise for the last year two years, with denials increasing from 5% to 8% of discharges. The hospital was also suffering from an increase in denied reimbursements of $550,000. Internal referrals to its home-care service had also declined in the last few months. Core Measure compliance performance was in the bottom quartile, well below the local competition.

Assessment and Findings

Alexis spent the first few months evaluating the units and attempting to formulate a discharge planning COS-Q (cost, operations, service, and quality of care) snapshot. The following is a summary of the additional information that she discovered.

Emergency Department (ED): The ED has just undergone redesign. According to their data, door-to-doc times are better than the national average. Additionally, diagnostic tests are reported in less than 45 minutes. The biggest barrier in the ED is obtaining a hospital bed. At times, a patient can be held in the ED for over 18 hours.

PACU: The Post-Anesthesia-Care Unit (PACU) is experiencing unprecedented capacity issues. At times, the unit is full and surgeries have to be canceled. The unit has focused on recovery times, and the average patient is in the PACU for 52 minutes. They also reviewed OR room turnover rate, which was under 30 minutes. After careful review, the data suggested the capacity issues were related to hospital census.

Environmental Services: Environmental services has just adopted a technology solution that pages an environmental specialist as soon as a patient is discharged. They then get to the room and completely turn the room around in under 30 minutes. Once the cleaning is completed, they immediately notify the unit supervisor, who in turn calls for the next admission.

Discharge Planning Department: The Discharge Planning Department is made up of case managers (10), social workers (10), and utilization-review members (15). The department operates Monday through Friday from 8 a.m. until 5 p.m.

- There are two types of case managers: physician-based and disease-based. The physician-based case managers are often tied to a physician group and do not participate in unit meetings. The disease-based case managers follow a specific patient population.

- Utilization-review nurses are unit based. Initial assessments demonstrated that the nurses have long tenure and follow their nursing judgment to dictate when they should address length-of-stay issues with a physician.

- Social workers see patients on a referral basis through a physician order. Only 17% of the patients at Hospital "A" are referred for post-acute-care service.

- There is little to no integration of this department. There are also five different job descriptions for three functions.

- The staffing plan varies on a day-to-day basis and is typically based on the preference of the staff members. Caseloads are assigned by unit and can vary from 5 to 25 cases per day.

- The utilization-review process includes a clinical-documentation program that was initiated in early 2000. To date, the program has only identified marginal opportunities for increased reimbursement, despite the fact that many of the diagnosis-related groups (DRGs) are low weighted, yet have a longer-than-average length of stay.

– The denial rate for utilization-review cases is very high. Approximately 8% of all inpatient cases are denied for lack of medical necessity. This often results in records having to be pulled after a patient had been discharged in an effort to prepare an appeal. In the last year, over $550,000 dollars was denied due to lack of medical necessity.

– The team members carry a folder filled with paperwork. All processes are manual and filing is labor intensive.

Team Culture: The discharge planning team members are among the longest tenured staff members. They have long-standing relationships with many of the doctors. They also have little to no accountability to the organization, not because they are not dedicated, but because they have never been asked to do things differently. When invited to an introductory meeting, they unanimously decided that they were among the most professional departments in the hospital. Further, they felt their process for discharge planning is among the best in the country. Two of the managers are certified as Six Sigma Green Belts, but the organization has never been able to successfully implement any projects.

Strategic Challenge

Alexis J. Simms picked up her presentation and began reviewing her recommendations. In the next 12 hours, the hospital executive leadership was to decide whether or not they could approve a redesign of this magnitude. While Alexis understood the task was a huge challenge, she also understood that not positioning the department to meet the coming challenges was a career-ending move. How do you think Alexis addressed the following issues?

1. What Performance Improvement methodology might work best in this environment?
2. How do you prioritize the issues?
3. Based on the current metrics, what are the weaknesses and strengths of the data?

4. What type of model for discharge planning is being used? What are the pros and cons?
5. What type of team configuration is being used? What are the pros and cons?
6. How do you rally the troops for change?
7. How would you begin to transition your team toward accountability?
8. Would technology benefit this organization?
9. On a high level, what do you think Alexis will recommend?

The Key

1. What methodology might be considered as one approach this issue?

   Although every organization should use the core principles of Lean and Six Sigma in all of their projects, in organizations with low tolerance for new process-improvement tools, it is critical to take incremental steps and start with the Lean–Six Sigma Action Workout. Once the departments have developed confidence, then the Green Belts can begin implementation of more statistically challenging projects. A secondary methodology is to just use Lean "visual workplace" solutions.

2. How do you prioritize the issues?

   The COS-Q snapshot is a great tool that assists with identifying priorities. The COS-Q snapshot is formatted to bring together metrics that have a relationship to other metrics in the quadrant. The snapshot provides leaders with the ability to compare outcomes data against all key metrics. Areas that are not performing as targeted, are more easily identified and therefore easier to prioritize.

3. Based on the current metrics, what are the strengths and weaknesses of the data?

   Strengths: Based on the assessment and findings, the Emergency Department, the PACU, and Environmental Service Departments are performing at an optimal level.
   Weaknesses: The data sets demonstrate a very narrow scope of information. As the COS-Q snapshot is reviewed, it is easy to notice

Table 13.1   Snapshot of COS-Q Discharge Planning Data

COSTS		OPERATIONS	
These are key financial metrics that impact the bottom line.		These are indications that show system efficiency	
Medical Necessity Data		Admit Trends Data	
Concurrent Denial Rate		ED Diversion Rate	?
Observation data		ED Hold Times	
Days saved		PACU Hold Times	?
Variance Data		Admission Delays	
Denial Data	?	Discharge Trends Data	
Cancelled Discharge		Bed Turn Over Data	?
		Average Length of Stay Data	?
SERVICE		QUALITY	
These are customer service scores as defined by both patients and physicians.		These are clinical measures that generally impact the patient care.	
Average Length of Discharge	?	Readmit Data	
Discharge Delay		Readmit Reason Data	
Initial DCP Assessment		Core Measure Compliance	?
Patient Satisfaction	?	Smoking Cessation	?
Physician Satisfaction	?	Influenza Vaccination	?
Referral Data	?	Pneumonia Vaccination	?

? denotes data that can be derived from information in the case study. The boxes that do not have a ? denote data that is unavailable or not recorded. This suggests that Hospital A may not track other key metrics that demonstrate discharge planning performance.

that most of the missing elements are discharge planning data (see Table 13.1).

4. What type of model for discharge planning is being used? What are the pros and cons?

Hospital "A" is using a triad model. This triad has case managers, utilization review, and social work team members.

Pros: There are more FTEs (full-time equivalents) to accomplish the tasks.

Cons: Often in a triad model there is redundancy in tasks. There also seems to be an overabundance of team members during the weekday and a shortage on the weekends.

5. What type of team configuration is being used? What are the pros and cons?

Hospital "A" uses unit-based, physician-based, and disease-based team configurations.
There are two types of case managers, physician-based and disease-based.

Pros: The benefit to using a physician-based or disease-based team configuration is the ability to have nurses focused on a specific disease or physician practice. This provides a key person that can keep up on best-practice guidelines as they develop.

Cons: At times, communication handoffs are compromised as the team members travel from unit to unit. Time is lost at elevators and stairways, and productivity is minimized. Additionally, when one person is on vacation or ill, there is no person with the same level of expertise to provide coverage, and therefore care can be compromised.

Utilization-review and social-worker team members are unit-based.

Pros: A unit-based model embraces Lean principles. This allows team members to be engaged in day-to-day operations. This model is further enhanced if the team member's clinical expertise can be aligned to the unit.

Cons: This model may not take full advantage of having a clinical expert driving best-practice standards.

6. How do you rally the troops for change?

In organizations with highly tenured staff members, it is nearly impossible to get large-scale changes in place without serious resistance. The best approach would be to make an effort to bring all staff on board, but not to spend too much time on those that are intent on just finishing the last few years before retirement. Begin this process by using the Change Matrix table in Chapter 9 to show the threats and opportunities of making or not making the change. This will lay out the logical reasons why change needs to occur. Additionally, it will provide insight into the team dynamics in the department.

7. How would you begin to transition your team toward accountability?

In order to build accountability, both system and team accountability must be fostered. System accountability requires that focus, influence, and consequences be discussed with the team members.

Focus: Team members must have clear expectations.
Influence: Team members must have influence over their work process and staff.
Consequences: Team members must recognize that there should be natural and logical consequences for all actions.

8. Would technology benefit this organization?

Yes, however technology should only be adopted after redesign. Current processes are antiquated with various staffing models. Once variation has been pulled out of the system, then technology can be implemented as an enhancement.

9. On a high level, what do you think Alexis will recommend?

Alexis must share a new vision of balancing COS-Q in the discharge planning process. Along with a new vision, she would need to share guiding principles that will set parameters for change. These principles are the Lean–Six Sigma methodologies. These will serve as the framework for change. She would begin with a current-state assessment and ask team members to participate in developing the vision for a future state.

- Use Lean to identify the model. (Lean thinking recommends a dyad model.)
- Use Lean to select team configuration. (Lean thinking recommends a unit-based model.)

- Adopt a standard guideline for medical necessity. A high denial rate that is attributed to medical necessity is typically related to the utilization-review process. Failure to provide a guideline results in inconsistent management of ALOS.
- Use DMAIC (define, measure, analyze, improve, and control) to aggressively identify denial issues. (The denial rate is very high, and this means lost revenue.)
- Use DMAIC to implement a Core Measure plan.
- Use DMAIC to address the CDMP (Clinical Documentation Management Program).
- Use DMAIC and scripting to implement a plan for gaining referrals.
- Implement a feedback mechanism to share success or failure. Rapidly address failure with a DMAIC process that recognizes success and rewards it.

Acronyms

5S	5S methodology: sort, set in order, shine, standardize, sustain	Chap. 5	p. 4
ACEI	angiotensin-converting enzyme inhibitor	Chap. 3	p. 10
ADT	admissions/discharges/transfers	Chap. 2	p. 6
ALOD	average length of discharge	Chap. 4	p. 3
ALOS	average length of stay	Chap. 1	p. 1
AMI	acute myocardial infarction	Chap. 2	p. 5
APC	ambulatory payment classifications	Chap. 6	p. 2
ARB	angiotensin receptor blocker	Chap. 3	p. 10
BSN	Bachelor of Science in Nursing	Chap. 7	p. 3
CAP	community-acquired pneumonia	Chap. 2	p. 5
CDC	Centers for Disease Control	Chap. 8	p. 1
CDMP	Clinical Documentation Management Program	Chap. 6	p. 4
CDR	clinical data repository	Chap. 2	p. 6
CEO	Chief Executive Officer	Chap. 7	p. 4
CM	case management	Chap. 2	p. 5
CMS	Centers for Medicare & Medicaid Services	Introduction	p. 2
COE	computerized order entry	Chap. 5	p. 5
COS-Q	cost, operations, service, and quality of care	Preface	p. 1
CPI	continuous process improvement	Chap. 5	p. 3
CQI	continuous quality improvement	Chap. 2	p. 1
CT	computed tomography	Chap. 6	p. 4

CTQ	critical to quality	Chap. 10	p. 2
DFSS	design for Six Sigma	Chap. 10	p. 2
DMAIC	define, measure, analyze, improve, and control	Preface	p. 1
DME	durable medical equipment	Chap. 2	p. 6
DPMO	defect per million opportunity	Chap. 10	p. 1
DRG	diagnosis-related group	Chap. 1	p. 2
DRIP	data rich–information poor	Chap. 2	p. 4
ECIN	extended-care information network	Chap. 1	p. 1
ED	emergency department	Introduction	p. 1
EGC	electrocardiogram	Chap. 3	p. 10
EMR	electronic medical record	Chap. 2	p. 2
FTE	full-time equivalent	Chap. 2	p. 4
HF	heart failure	Chap. 2	p. 5
HQID	hospital quality incentive demonstration	Introduction	p. 2
ICU	intensive care unit	Chap. 3	p. 11
IDS	integrated delivery system	Chap. 1	p. 2
IHI	Institute for Healthcare Improvement	Chap. 5	p. 1
IOM	Institute of Medicine	Chap. 5	p. 3
IPPS	inpatient prospective payment system	Chap. 6	p. 3
IT	information technology	Chap. 2	p. 6
JIT	just in time	Chap. 5	p. 2
LBBB	left-bundle branch block	Chap. 3	p. 10
LOS	length of stay	Chap. 2	p. 2
LVEF	left ventricular ejection fraction	Chap. 3	p. 11
LVF	left ventricular function	Chap. 3	p. 10
LVSD	left ventricular systolic dysfunction	Chap. 3	p. 10
MI	myocardial infarction	Chap. 4	p. 3
MRI	magnetic resonance imaging	Chap. 5	p. 2
MS-DRG	Medicare severity-adjusted diagnosis-related groups	Chap. 6	p. 3

NRC	National Research Corporation	Chap. 4	p. 5
OPPS	Outpatient Prospective Payment System	Chap. 6	p. 2
PACS	Picture Archiving and Communication Systems	Chap. 5	p. 4
PACU	postanesthesia-care unit	Chap. 3	p. 2
PCI	percutaneous coronary intervention	Chap. 3	p. 10
PCP	primary care provider	Chap. 2	p. 6
PFP	pay-for-performance	Chap. 2	p. 3
PI	performance improvement	Chap. 2	p. 1
PMI	Project Management Institute	Chap. 2	p. 1
PN	pneumonia	Chap. 3	p. 11
POD	postoperative day	Chap. 3	p. 12
PTCA	percutaneous transluminal coronary angioplasty	Chap. 3	p. 10
RFP	request for proposal	Chap. 9	p. 4
RN	registered nurse	Chap. 3	p. 4
ROI	return on investment	Chap. 2	p. 1
RVU	relative-value unit	Chap. 2	p. 4
SCIP	Surgical Care Improvement Project	Chap. 2	p. 5
TPS	Toyota Production System	Chap. 5	p. 2
TQM	Total Quality Management	Chap. 2	p. 1
UR	utilization review	Chap. 2	p. 7
VSM	Value Stream Mapping	Chap. 5	p. 5
WHPPD	worked hours per patient day	Chap. 2	p. 4
WIP	work in progress	Chap. 5	p. 3
WLU	workload unit	Chap. 2	p. 4

Bibliography

Axis Performance Advisors. 1997. The accountability hot potato.
http://home.pacifier.com/~axis/T6potato.html.

Bazzoli, G., et al. 2003. Does U.S. hospital capacity need to be expanded? *Health Affairs* 22 (6): 40–54.

Benbow, D., and T. M. Kubiak. 2005. *The Certified Six Sigma Black Belt Handbook.* Milwaukee: ASQ Quality Press.

Berrett, B., et al. 2007. Ready or not, customer service is coming to healthcare. White paper for The Beryl Institute.

Bridges, W. 1991. *Managing transitions: Making the most of change.* Reading, Mass.: Perseus Books.

Brunner, F. 2005. Be interactive, not reactive or proactive. http://ezinearticles.com/?Be-interactive,-Not-Reactive-or-Proactive&id=73519&opt=print.

Chartis Group and American Hospital Association. Prepared to care: Providing 24-hour access to care. http://www.caringforcommunities.org/caringfor-communities/content/preparedtocare.pdf.

Covey, S. R. 1990. The 7 Habits of Highly Effective People. *New York: Simon & Schuster.*

DeFrances, C. J., and M. J. Hall. 2007. 2005 national hospital discharge survey. Centers for Disease Control. www.cdc.gov/nchs/data/ad/ad385.pdf.

Flanagan, S., and A. Kjesbo. 2004. Conquering capacity: By improving its patient flow, one hospital has been able to admit an additional 400 patients since January 2003 and expects to maintain that potential. *Healthcare Financial Manage.* 58 (7): 92–96.

Gale Group. 2004. Medical necessity denials: Prevention pays off. *Healthcare Financial Manage.* 58 (10).

Grey, L. 2001. Readmission of patients to hospital: Still ill-defined and poorly understood. *Int. J. Qual. Health Care* 13 (3): 177–179.

Hammer, D. C. 2006. Adapting customer service to consumer-directed health care. *Healthcare Financial Manage.* 60 (9).

Healthcare Advisory Board. 2001. The new economics of care: Briefing for the board and health systems executives. Washington, D.C.: Advisory Board Company.

Jacks, R. 2003. Six Sigma: PDCA on steroids? *iSixSigma Healthcare Newsl.* 1 (10). http://healthcare.isixsigma.com/library/content/c030624a.asp.

Joint Commission. www.jointcommission.org/performancestandards.

Kirby, A. 2003. Patient flow product taps hidden capacity: Up to 20% increase in bed capacity possible. *Healthcare Benchmarks Qual. Improvement* 10 (12): 139–141.

Kirby, A., and A. Kjesbo. 2003. Tapping into hidden hospital bed capacity. *Healthcare Financial Manage.* 57 (11): 38–41.

Kloehn, P. 2004. Demystifying patient throughput to optimize revenue & patient satisfaction. White Paper for Zimmerman, Hales Corner, Wis. http://www.healthleadersmedia.com/print.cfm?content_id=54416&parent=103.

Landro, L. 2007. Keeping patients from landing back in the hospital. *The Wall Street Journal Online* (December 12). http://online.wsj.com/public/article_print/SB119741713239122065.html.

Leary, R., and D. Farley. 2007. Surviving Medicare's IPPS changes: What you need to know. *Healthcare Financial Manage.* 61 (12): 48–55.

Martinez, R, T. Buchman, and M. Roizen. 2006. Report slams U.S. emergency care system. Interview on *Talk of the Nation*, NPR, June 14, 2006. www.npr.org/templates/story/story.php?storyId=5485128.

Miller, D., and T. Merryman. 2005. Medical surgical innovation community: Lean thinking. Powerpoint presentation. Institute for Healthcare Improvement. http://hfrp.umm.edu/workflow/MD2_Lean.pdf.

NRC Picker. 2007. Case study: Integrating measurement and improvement. http://nrcpicker.com/Default.aspx?DN=21,2,1,Documents.

Pearson, S. D., D. Goulart-Fisher, and T. H. Lee. 1995. Critical pathways as a strategy for improving care: Problems and potential. *Ann. Intern. Med.* 123: 941–948.

Pexton, C. 2003. Confronting a national dilemma: Overcrowding, delays and diversion in the emergency department. White paper for GE Medical Systems. http://www.gehealthcare.com/usen/service/docs/ed_monograph_finalhr.pdf.

Pexton, C., and D. Young. 2004. Reducing surgical site infections through Six Sigma and change management. *Patient Safety Qual. Healthcare* (July/Sept.). http://www.psqh.com/julsep04/pextonyoung.html.

Phipps, R. 2006. Lean & Six Sigma in healthcare. Presented at Aramco Services Co., ASQ Section 1405. http://www.asqhouston.org/rphipps.pdf.

Premier, Inc. 2008. CMS/premier hospital quality demonstration. http://www.premierinc.com/quality-safety/tools-services/p4p/hqi/index.jsp.

Sawyer, B. 2007. Effective discharge begins at admission. White paper for Patient Placement Systems.

Six Sigma Lean Newsletter. 2004. Can Six Sigma cure healthcare? Physicians, hospitals increasingly prescribe quality Rx. *6σL Newsl.* 1 (1): 5–7. http://www.gehealthcare.com/usen/service/docs/six_sigma_cure.pdf.

Terra, S. 2007. An evidence-based approach to case management model selection for an acute care facility: Is there really a preferred model? *Professional Case Management* 12 (3): 147–157.

Washington State Hospital Association. 2006. Integrated delivery systems. In *Governing Board Orientation Manual*, chap. 11. http://www.wsha.org/files/62/Gov_Bd_Manual_INTEGRATED.doc.

Wikipedia. Accountability. http://en.wikipedia.org/wiki/Accountability.

Willard, M. 1997. The accountability hot potato. Axis Performance Advisors, Inc. http://home.pacifier.com/~axis/T6potato.html.

Youngstrom, N. 2005. Admission medical-necessity errors abound: Hospitals try new compliance strategies. *Report on Medicare Compliance* 14 (10). http://www.lhcr.org/PDF/HPMPWorkBook/AppU_ReportMedicareCompliance.pdf.

Index

Authors

Ali Birjandi, MBA, MHA, CPHIMS, ASQ SSBB, is currently a vice president of operational performance improvement. He has a BS in operations management, with an MBA and an MHA from the University of Florida.

With more than 15 years experience in management engineering, Mr. Birjandi has worked in various organizations from acute care facilities to vertically integrated multihospital systems. Throughout his career he has worked diligently both at local levels and on the national stage to assist colleagues to become more efficient and productive. Using data to drive efficiency is his passion, and creating the *Discharge Planning Handbook for Healthcare* was an opportunity to show how modern Lean and data-driven tools can identify significant opportunities.

He is an American Society of Quality-certified Six Sigma Black Belt and carries the HIMSS CPHIMS certification. He has been published in various healthcare journals and has made numerous presentations in national conferences.

To contact the author, send emails to birjandi@yahoo.com.

Lisa M. Bragg, RN, BSN, MBA, has enjoyed the healthcare arena for over 17 years. She earned the RN from the Medical College of Ohio, a BSN from Bowling Green State University, and a MBA from the University of Toledo. As a former utilization review nurse, case manager, and discharge planner, Lisa was inspired to assist colleagues in understanding the critical importance of these functions. It was her belief that these professional roles are not well understood and are underutilized and underestimated. It is her hope that *Discharge Planning Handbook for Healthcare* will serve as a new platform that provokes healthcare leaders to change the way they look at members of the discharge planning team.

Aside from her professional career, Lisa has served in the U.S. Army as a National Guard member for the 385th Medical Company for eight years. There, she learned the value of standardization, attention to detail, and the value of focused, concerted action.

In 2006, Lisa was appointed as the project manager in one of America's most integrated healthcare systems, implementing a discharge planning technology solution for nine hospitals, eight skilled nursing facilities, and a home-care division. She currently serves as an administrative director for eight senior-service facilities, a regional call center, and a private-duty nurse division.

She is the co-founder of IPD Health Solutions and hopes to begin consulting for hospitals across the country.

To contact the author, send emails to lisa.bragg@yahoo.com.